MW01626258

WHERE GOD CAME DOWN

The Archaeological Evidence

WHERE GOD CAME DOWN

The Archaeological Evidence

Joel P. Kramer

All black & white photographs appearing in this book are from the Matson (G. Eric and Edith) Photograph Collection, a rich archive of historical photographs of the Middle East mainly taken between 1898–1946.

Editing by Cathy Kramer

Special thanks for editing assistance:
Carissa Flores, Eric Johnson & Susan Dorsey Sivadon

Additional thanks for editing and layout work:
Rachael Carrington & Bart Dahmer
www.innovopublishing.com

Printed in the United States of America, U.S.
Printing History, First Edition: 2020
14 13 12 11 10 SP 27 26 25

Published by Expedition Bible—an imprint of Sourceflix Inc.
P. O. Box 606
Brigham City, Utah 84302
www.ExpeditionBible.com
visit: www.WhereGodCameDown.com

Publisher's Cataloging in Publication data

Names: Kramer, Joel P., author.

Title: Where God came down : the archaeological evidence / Joel P. Kramer.

Description: Brigham City, Utah : Expedition Bible, [2020] | Includes bibliographical references and index.

Identifiers: ISBN: 978-0-9980374-1-7 (hardbound) | 978-0-9980374-2-4 (softbound) | LCCN: 2019905698

Subjects: LCSH: Bible--Antiquities. | Bible--Historiography. | Bible--Evidences, authority, etc. | Bible--History of Biblical events. | Jesus Christ--Historicity. | Jesus Christ--Biography-- Sources. | Jesus Christ--Biography--History and criticism. | Christian antiquities. | Middle East--Antiquities. | Middle East--History--To 622. | Excavations (Archaeology)--Middle East. | Palestine--Antiquities. | Palestine--History--To 70 A.D. | Bible. Old Testament--History of Biblical events. | Bible. New Testament--Criticism, interpretation, etc. | Bible. New Testament --History of Biblical events. | BISAC: RELIGION / Antiquities & Archaeology. | RELIGION / Biblical Criticism & Interpretation / General.

Classification: LCC: BS621 .K73 2020 | DDC: 220.9/3--dc23

CONTENTS

INTRODUCTION

Mention the word *archaeology*, and people often conjure up images of digging under a blazing desert sun and unearthing an ancient treasure trove. Talk about biblical archaeology, and topics like the Ark of the Covenant or chariot wheels at the bottom of the Red Sea frequently make their way into the conversation. But aside from potential riches and sensational finds, the real purpose of archaeology is to gain an understanding of past cultures by studying what they left behind: their pottery, tools, buildings, graves, bones, etc.

We moderns tend to put a lot of confidence in what we think archaeology can tell us. There is a collective sense that archaeology knows the truth about the past. But how does it know? How can anything much be known from pieces of pottery, scraps of metal, fallen stones, or brittle bones?

In addition to picks and spades, ancient texts have traditionally been used by archaeologists as critically important tools to gain a clear understanding of the past they are uncovering. Writings that come from antiquity about people, places, and events are necessary to be able to understand and interpret rather than just speculate about what comes out of the ground.

In the field of biblical archaeology, there is one ancient text in particular that is crucial to accurately understand the archaeological record. That ancient text is the Bible. Unfortunately, it is a growing reality that biblical archaeology is a very secular field, increasingly choosing to reject the Bible as a source of information.

There are some exceptions, however. In his book The Archaeology of Ancient Israel, well-known and respected Israeli archaeologist Dr. Amnon Ben-Tor writes, "Eliminate the Bible from the archaeology of the Land of Israel . . . and you have deprived it of its soul." If you eliminate the Bible, you lose the ability to accurately draw meaning from what archaeology uncovers.

To better grasp the working relationship between the Bible and archaeology, consider the following analogy. A five-hundred-piece jigsaw puzzle box is found with only five pieces inside: one percent of the jigsaw puzzle remains, the rest of the pieces are lost. Those few pieces are important evidence supporting the reality that at one time, the whole puzzle existed.

But what can be done with only five pieces out of a five-hundred-piece puzzle? Practically nothing. There is one help, however. The box lid is still intact, and it shows a picture of the whole puzzle. Equipped with this bigger picture, we can now see where the five pieces fit in to their larger context. In biblical archaeology, the five puzzle pieces represent the archaeology—what comes up out of the ground—while the picture on the front of the box represents the role of the Bible.

In Israel, of all the land area that could potentially be excavated, only about one percent has been. That small percentage of archaeological evidence can't tell us much. What is necessary to interpret the excavated material is the bigger picture that the Bible provides; it is the critical key to understanding the archaeology of the biblical lands.

Unfortunately, archaeologists holding to an authoritative view of Scripture represent an extreme minority in a field dominated by secular scholars. The disagreement between biblical and secular worldviews is not so much over evidence and facts but rather how to interpret the evidence and what explains the facts. An archaeologist who does not believe in God, miracles, or the supernatural will inevitably interpret archaeology differently than one who does.

This book does not attempt to find agreement between the two opposing belief systems. Rather, it carefully focuses on using the Bible to understand what has been found in the ground and, beyond that, to seek the spiritual significance that can be gleaned from that understanding.

Second Timothy 3:16 says, "All Scripture is God-breathed and is useful for teaching." And in John 5:39 Jesus declares, "These are the very Scriptures that testify about me." In the pages that follow, we will explore ten specific places spoken of in the Bible. These places all have something in common—Jesus was there. He stood on some of these sites in a preincarnate manifestation and on others wearing the flesh of humanity. These ten sites are all part of the earthly landscape of redemption's story. They are the places ... *Where God Came Down.*

PART I

OLD TESTAMENT

HOLY PLACES

Exposed ruins can be seen in the bottom-left of this aerial photo. Tel Hebron is in the distance, less than two miles away. (photo looks to the south)

Chapter 1

THE PLACE OF PROMISES

In this first chapter I want to put our jigsaw puzzle analogy into practice. First we will look at the archaeology of the site without knowing the identification of the site with certainty, having only the "few pieces" found in the ground. Examining the archaeology alone will put you, the reader, in the same position as an archaeologist who is digging through the layers, asking questions, and trying to interpret all the findings.

Next we will turn to the Bible and other ancient historical texts to illuminate our understanding of what has been discovered. Those texts will provide the bigger picture needed to properly interpret the evidence unearthed at the site. Sometimes specific verses will bring out specific meaning, and sometimes an overall history recorded in a book or document will provide a breadth of important historical context.

Finally, we will examine how the Bible and archaeology complement one another and see how archaeology presents evidence that even critics of the Bible cannot easily dismiss.

Now, without stating its identity, let me introduce you to our first excavation site.

THE ARCHAEOLOGY ALONE

This ancient mound is called Ramet Haram Al-Khalil, which in Arabic means "The Height of the Sanctuary of the Friend." It was first excavated in 1926–1928 by a German archaeologist named Evaristus Mader and then again in 1984–1986 by Israeli archaeologist Yitzhak Magen.[1] Of these two excavations, Mader's was by far the most extensive. His team exposed one archaeological layer at a time, and in those layers they found remains of structures, artifacts, and an abundance of pottery. Archaeologists use pottery to date archaeological layers. Because styles of pottery change over time, determining when these changes took place provides general dates for the layers in which the pottery was found. To give you an idea, imagine figuring out the general date of a photograph by looking at car models, hairstyles, and clothing styles within the picture.

Similarly, different pottery styles gave Mader a basic understanding of the various time periods in which the site was occupied. The oldest pottery he found dated to the Bronze Age (c. 2000 BC), establishing that the site had been occupied as far back as four thousand years ago.[2] Supporting this finding was the fact that the site had a natural spring, still active today, which would have provided a water source for the people and their animals. So the important question Mader had to ask was, *Who lived there four thousand years ago?* Based on the archaeology alone, it was impossible to know.

Once the members of Mader's team reached bedrock, they could dig no deeper. The bedrock itself, however, revealed something interesting: several large, round holes piercing them straight through. The team was left with the question, *What caused these holes?*

Img. 1: Mader's excavations in the 1920s, near Hebron.

When they examined the center of the site, all that remained were a few stones which seemed to form the corner of a structure (see *Img. 3*). However, similar to having only a few puzzle pieces to go by, those few stones were not enough to enable the team to determine what kind of structure had been erected there.

In the next layer above the bedrock and therefore later in time (moving upward from bedrock is like moving to the right on a timeline), Mader uncovered the remains of two square, stone structures next to each other, near the southwest corner of the site. The embedded pottery dated the structures to the Iron Age (1000–586 BC). Again, based on the archaeology alone, identifying the purpose of these structures would have been pure conjecture: Bathrooms? Houses? Storage areas?

Above the Iron Age layer was a later layer (still moving to the right on a timeline) dating to the Early Roman Period (63 BC–AD 70). This layer included massive walls (which still enclose the site today). Pottery and other small finds embedded in these walls dated their construction to the first century BC. As impressive as these walls were, in and of themselves they couldn't provide answers to basic questions: Who built them? For what purpose?

Mader found evidence within the walls, indicating that they had been renovated in the Late Roman Period (second century AD). Later, in the Byzantine Period (AD 324–638), a building was constructed inside the older enclosure walls. Could the ruins of this building help determine who built it?

Above the Byzantine level was the top-most layer which Mader dug first. It consisted of scattered walls dating to the Islamic Period (which began in AD 638). Why did Muslims build here?

So, from the top layer down to bedrock, the archaeology Mader unearthed couldn't reveal answers to critical questions: What is this site? Why, in this particular place, is there one thing built on top of another over such a long period of time? What is the link from four thousand years ago that carries through to today?

Historical context—details about this place from the distant past—was needed for accurate understanding. What could provide those details? An ancient text. If an archaeologist doesn't have an ancient source to use in identifying and understanding a site, his findings are speculation, with no solid verification.

Fortunately, Mader did have an ancient text to aid his understanding and interpretation—the Bible. As we will see in the following section, using the Bible, and particularly the book of Genesis, Mader was able to clearly identify the site he was excavating as Mamre, the ancient campsite of Abraham.

Img. 2: Surrounded by the city of Hebron, this site (center) was a mound of dirt-covered ruins until Mader's excavations cleared it down to the bedrock.

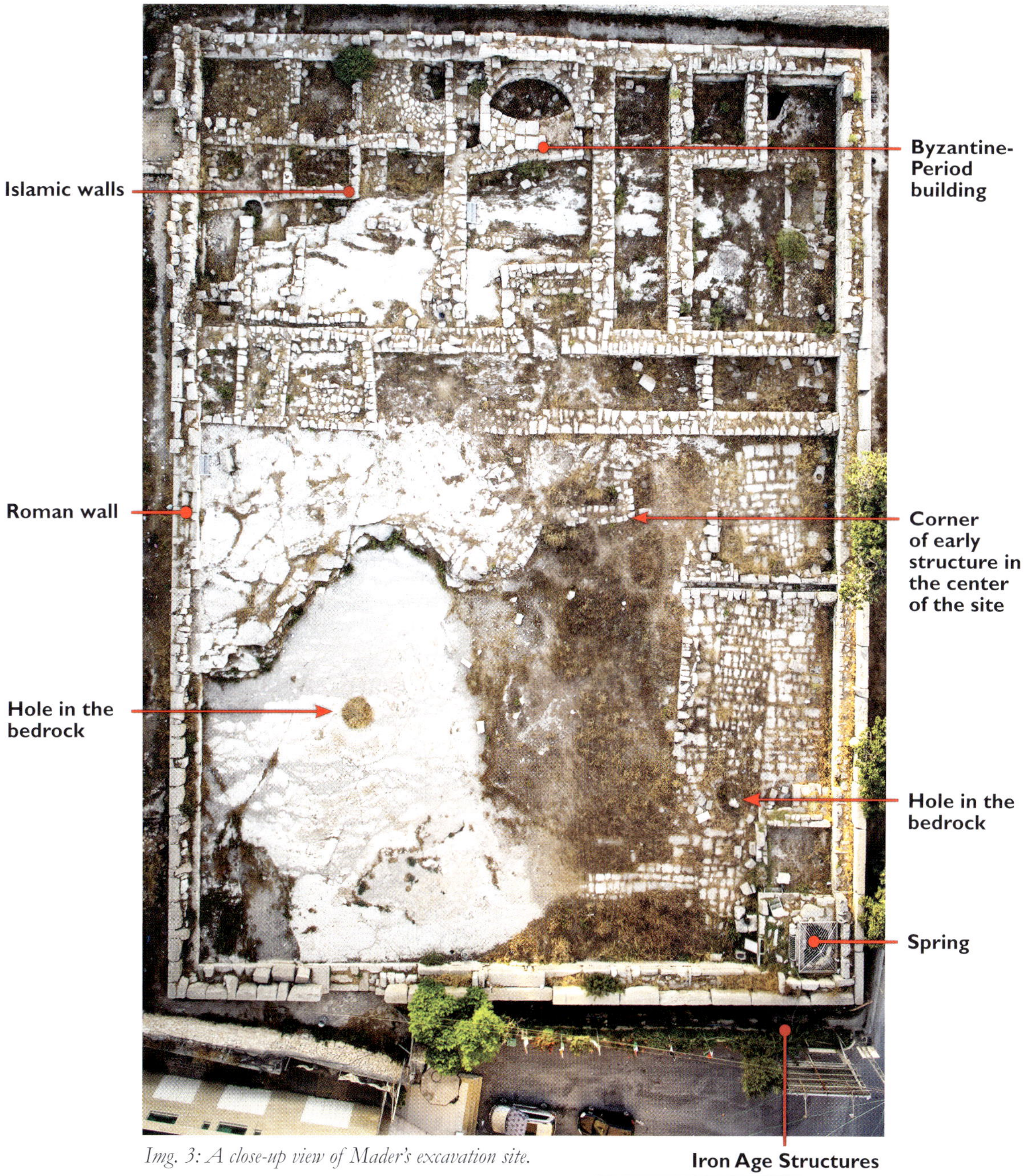

Img. 3: A close-up view of Mader's excavation site.

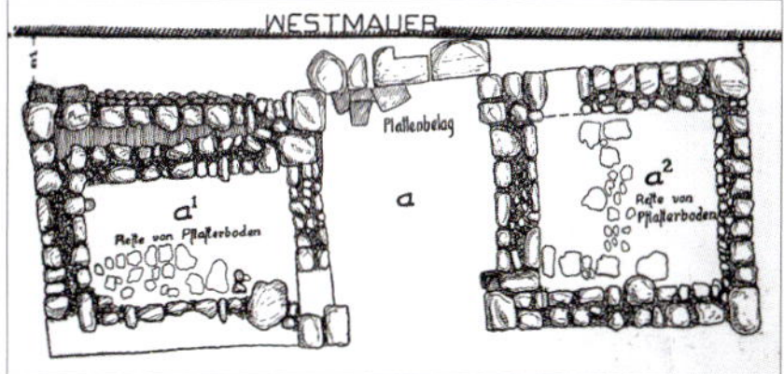

Img. 4: These are drawings of the Iron Age structures in Mader's excavation report. The connecting red line points to where the two structures were found outside Mamre's wall. These structures have been paved over and are no longer visible.

BIBLICAL AND EXTRA-BIBLICAL TEXTS

Layer 1

TIME OF ABRAHAM (2000 BC)

Genesis is the oldest text mentioning Mamre. The name first appears in Genesis 13:18: "So Abram (later renamed Abraham) went to live near the great trees of Mamre at Hebron, where he pitched his tents. There he built an altar to the LORD."

This one short verse lays a strong foundation for understanding the archaeology we've been discussing. The location of Mamre was at Hebron. Notice it does not say *in* but rather *at* Hebron. Because the Bible describes Abram as a nomad with large herds of animals, it makes sense that he wouldn't live within the walls of the city but rather on the surrounding land, outside of Hebron. Located just a few miles from Hebron, Mader's site fits well with this biblical description.

Img. 5: Close to the ruins of Tel Hebron, Mamre is located on the east side of the ancient road that connected Hebron with Jerusalem.

By mentioning "the great trees of Mamre," this verse also provides context which explains the deep holes Mader's team found. In the rocky terrain of the Middle East, trees often grow up through bedrock, and long after the trees themselves have died and rotted away, holes remain, marking the spot where they stood. Additionally, these tree holes were near what Mader called "Abraham's Spring."[3] Having a constant water source would have enabled these trees to flourish and become "great trees."

Imgs. 6 and 7 (above left and right): The tree rings at Mamre are still identifiable where they penetrated the bedrock.

Img. 8: A spring was Mamre's 's main water source in the time of Abraham. It has now been turned into a well and covered over with a metal grate.

Genesis 13:18 also tells us that although Abram was a nomad, he did actually build something at Mamre: "There he built an altar to the LORD." Based on the information in this verse, Mader marked the center of his excavation plan with the letter "J" and labeled it "Foundations of Abraham's Altar."[4] We will wait to see why Mader believed this was the precise spot where Abraham built his altar, because his reasoning is based on archaeological evidence which we will examine shortly. The point for now is that Mader did not have to guess whether there had been an altar built at Mamre four thousand years ago. He knew it to be a reality based on the biblical text.

One final, obvious thing we glean from Genesis 13:18 is that Abram lived at Mamre. And, the archaeological evidence concurs. Bronze Age pottery found on the site established that it was occupied at the time of Abraham, around 2000 BC.[5] This period is in line with the biblical dates for Abraham.[6]

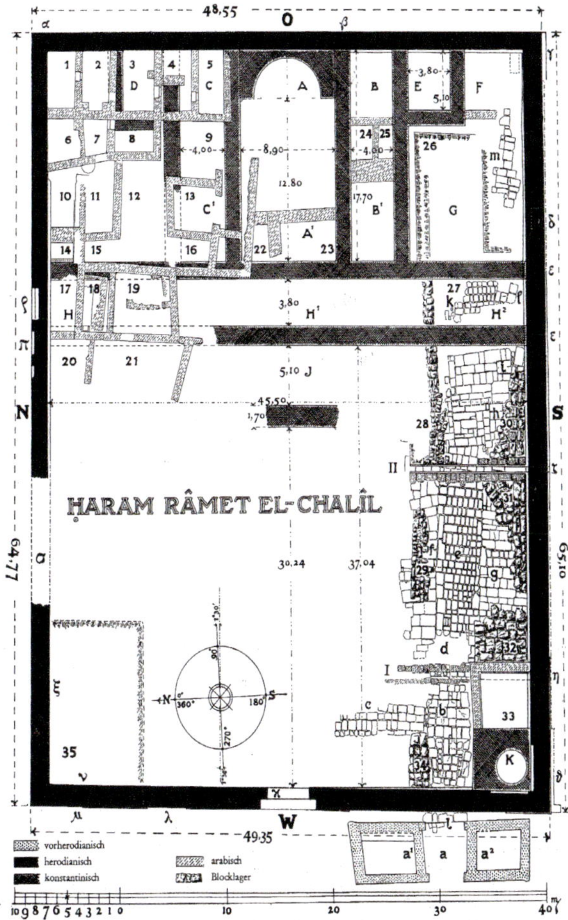

Img. 9: Mader's excavation plan of Mamre. Note the letter "J" (center, circled in red), marking the place Mader referred to as the "Foundations of Abraham's Altar."

Img. 10: A close-up of the center of Mamre; note the visible corner where the stones are exposed.

This one verse gives enough information to understand a significant amount about Mader's site. It paints a picture of Abram encamped at an ideal location, with water and shade for his family and livestock, having built an altar. But Genesis goes on to describe the big picture (to use our puzzle example), offering more information which will help to answer why this site continued to be venerated through the centuries.

The Bible tells the story of the event that occurred at Mamre, which changed it from a mere campsite to a place marked and honored thousands of years later:

> The Lord appeared to Abraham near the great trees of Mamre while he was sitting at the entrance to his tent in the heat of the day. Abraham looked up and saw three men standing nearby. When he saw them, he hurried from the entrance of his tent to meet them and bowed low to the ground. . . . Then one of them said, "I will surely return to you about this time next year, and Sarah your wife will have a son." Now Sarah was listening at the entrance to the tent, which was behind him. Abraham and Sarah were already very old, and Sarah was past the age of childbearing. So Sarah laughed to herself as she thought, "After I am worn out and my lord is old, will I now have this pleasure?" Then the Lord said to Abraham, "Why did Sarah laugh and say, 'Will I really have a child, now that I am old?' Is anything too hard for the Lord? I will return to you at the appointed time next year, and Sarah will have a son." Sarah was afraid, so she lied and said, "I did not laugh." But he said, "Yes, you did laugh." . . . Then the Lord said, "Shall I hide from Abraham what I am about to do? Abraham will surely become a great and powerful nation and all nations on earth will be blessed through him." (Genesis 18:1-2, 10-15, 17-18)

What makes the site of Mamre profound? The Lord stood there and conversed with Abraham. Mamre is holy ground.

The last verse in the above passage states that God told Abraham he would "become" something

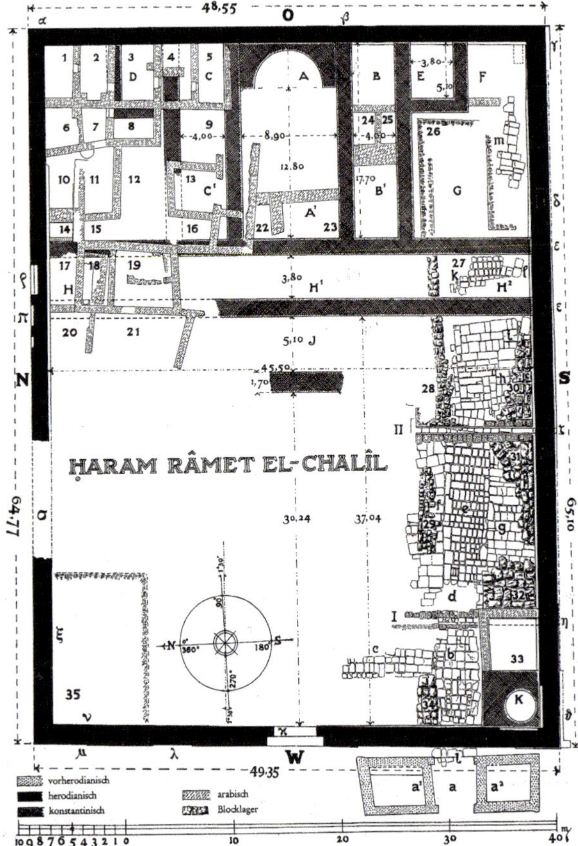

Img. 11: Mader's original top plan of Mamre.

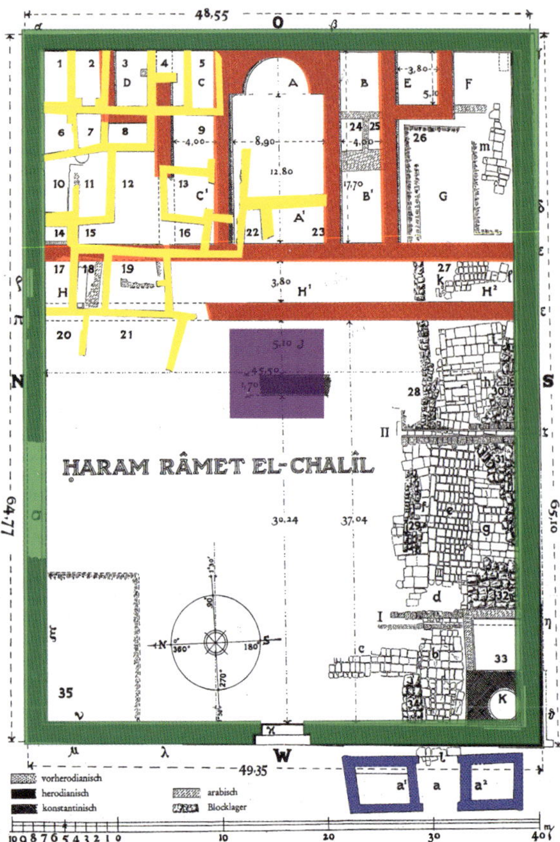

Img. 12: Mader's plan, overlaid with different colors to identify the structures of each occupation layer.

Img. 13: A simplified, color-coded plan of the excavation layers.

MAMRE'S LAYERS

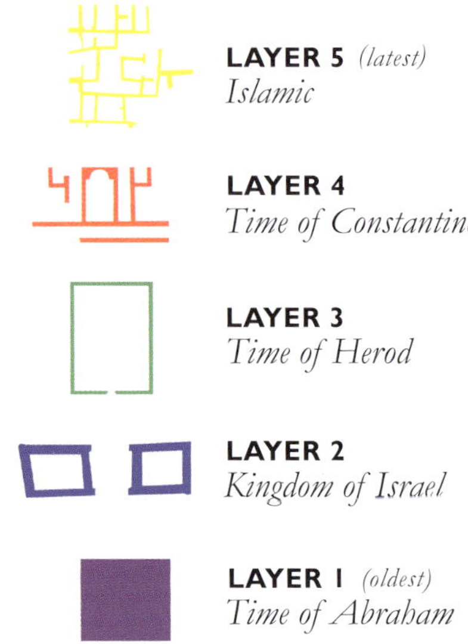

Img. 14: This is a key to the color-coded layers.

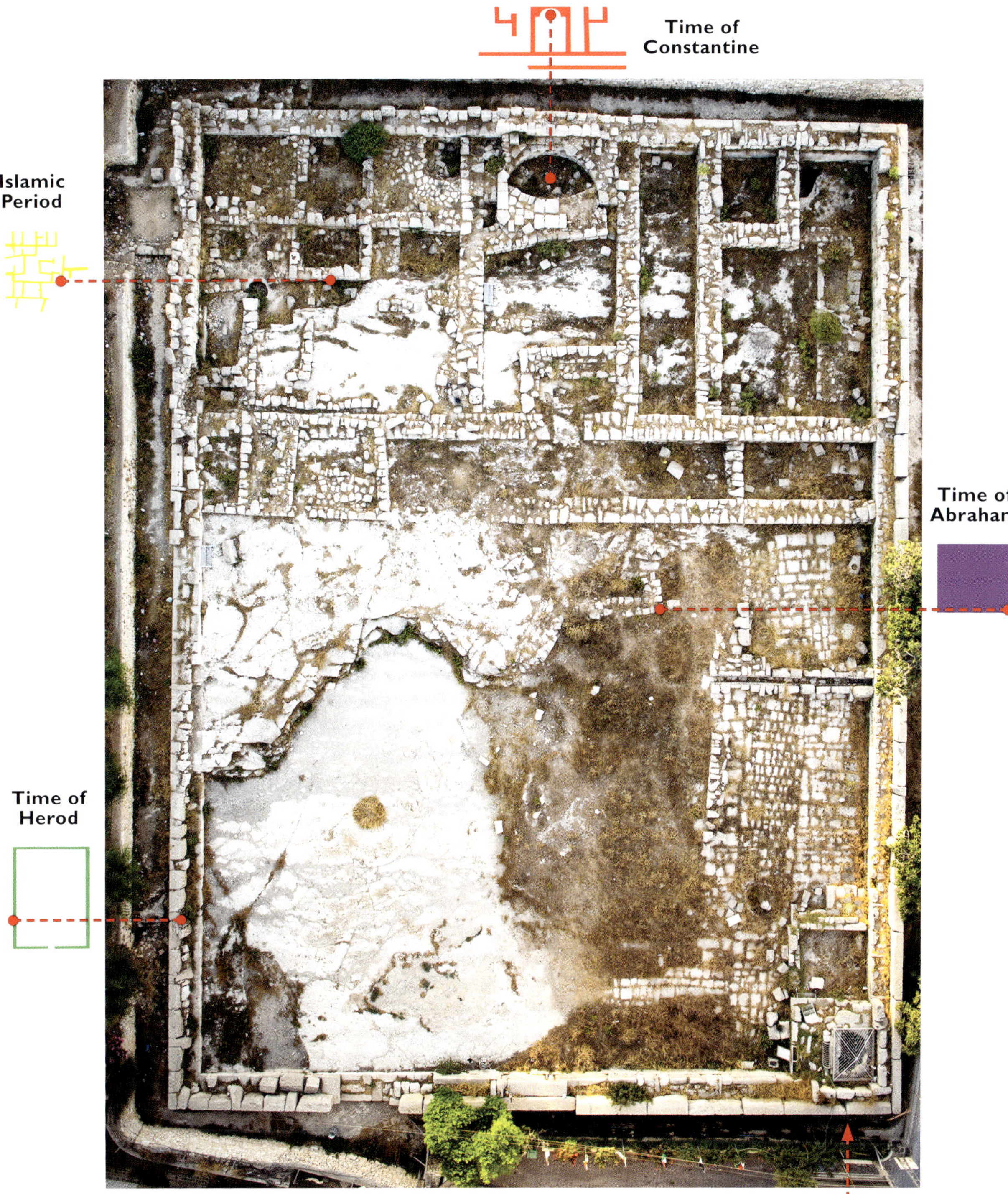

Img. 15: An aerial view of Mamre as it looks today, showing location of each color-coded layer.

more than what he then was. This word become is critical for understanding the site of Mamre, because over time the site itself will also become more than the campsite it was in Abraham's day.

First the Lord promised Abraham he would "become a great and powerful nation." That is an extraordinary promise to give to a very old, sonless man living in a tent with a barren wife. Is there any evidence that such a promise came true? We will continue to explore each of the archaeological layers in order to answer that question.

Layer 2

KINGDOM OF ISRAEL PERIOD (1000–586 BC)

In this layer, Mader unearthed two square structures with a passage between them. He identified those structures as being two sides of a gate dating to the Iron Age (1000–586 BC).[7] The dating of this gate established that it was in use during the time when kings ruled over the nation of Israel.

The gate Mader found was only a small part of a larger structure that was no longer standing. Finding incomplete structural remains is the norm in excavations because previous structures are often destroyed by later building projects. Stones from earlier walls are often reused to construct newer ones.

Despite this robbing out of building materials, pieces and portions of earlier structures are often preserved in archaeological layers. However small, these structural remnants are significant because they provide evidence for the existence of the larger construction they once belonged to.

Such is the case with the stone structures Mader found near the spring at Mamre. They represent a gate that once led in to an enclosure surrounding the site. Just as a single piece of pottery speaks to the whole pot it once belonged to, so too the parts of this gate speak to the reality that in the Kingdom of Israel Period, there was an enclosure surrounding the sacred site of Mamre.

Why would the Kingdom of Israel build walls to protect and commemorate Mamre? Because their own Scriptures, the Old Testament, informed them that this was the plot of ground where the LORD had appeared and made a promise to Abraham which ensured their very existence.

Img. 16: Photo taken by Mader showing the two stone structures of the Israelite-Period gate.

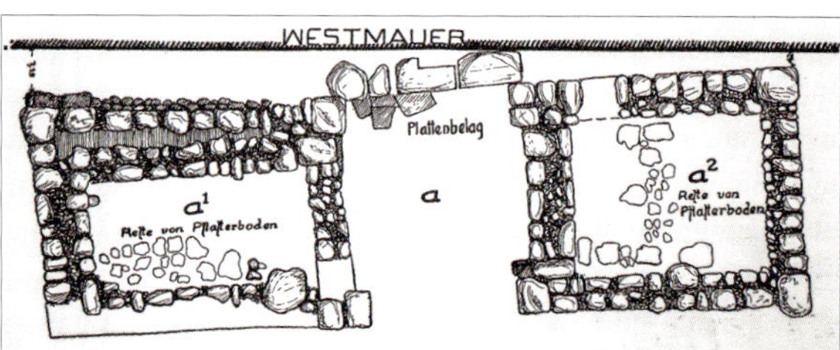

Img. 17: A drawing of the same stone structures identified in Mader's excavation report.

Img. 18: The grey dashed line represents what would have been an Israelite-Period enclosure surrounding the altar area. All that Mader found of this ancient enclosure was the gate that once led into it, which is enough to indicate that the enclosure existed.

Layer 3

TIME OF HEROD THE GREAT (First Century BC)

The next archaeological layer to examine, still visible today, is made up of the enclosure walls which Herod built when he came into power. Unfortunately, during this construction, the previous Israelite enclosure was destroyed.

Herod's walls were made of large cut stones. Pottery and other small finds date the construction of these walls to the first century BC, when the New Testament texts say that Herod the Great ruled as king over Judea. In addition to the Bible, Flavius Josephus, a Jewish-Roman historian, also attests to Herod's rule in the late first century AD.

Most of Herod's actions did not reflect the moniker of "Great." However, there is one area where he lived up to his name—he was a great builder, responsible for numerous large-scale building projects. While neither the Bible nor Josephus state specifically that Herod built up Mamre, the masonry style at Mamre matches several other sites which Herod built.[8]

Although Herod's monumental walls wiped out most of what had previously stood, their existence served to preserve the site and their placement helped to identify the site's focus—Abraham's altar. It was the centerpiece, enshrined at the center, surrounded by massive walls. In all of Judea, Herod built up only three sites in order to please his Jewish subjects.[9] The fact that one of them was Mamre demonstrates its significance as an important Jewish holy site.

Mader's interpretation of this layer was that the site had been built up over time around a central altar. Later excavations at Mamre led archaeologist Yitzhak Magen to agree with Mader's finding.[10]

It is unlikely that the altar which stood at the center of Herod's enclosure was used for sacrifices. Instead it was solely commemorative; because, according to Jewish law, the altar at the temple in Jerusalem was the only place where sacrifices could be legitimately offered. To sacrifice on any other altar would have been seen as blasphemous by the Jews of Herod's day.

Img. 19: These Herodian walls still surround the site of Mamre. This photo was taken not long after the excavations.

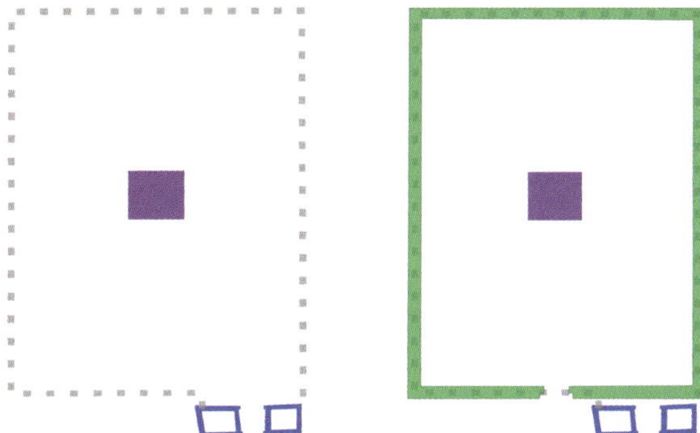

Img. 20: Outline of Israelite-Period enclosure (left) which, other than the gate, was totally destroyed when Herod built his monumental enclosure (right).

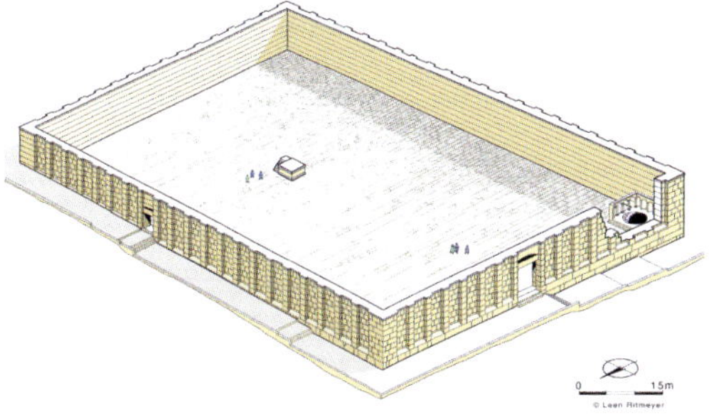

Img. 21: Leen Ritmeyer's reconstruction of Herod's enclosure and the altar it commemorated. The altar was later desecrated by pagan sacrifices.

Layer 4

TIME OF CONSTANTINE (Fourth Century AD)

Next, Mader excavated the foundations of a building dating to the Byzantine Period. There is no need to guess its purpose because we have direct source texts explaining the reasons and instructions for its construction.

In AD 324 Constantine defeated his pagan rival, Licinius, to become the sole ruler over a united Roman Empire. Now, for the first time, Mamre was under the control of a Roman emperor who proclaimed Christian faith. Not long after he consolidated power, Constantine's mother-in-law, Eutropia, visited Mamre on a pilgrimage to the Holy Land. She wrote to her son-in-law about the pagan worship practices she observed there.

Img. 22: Constantine

In response, Constantine wrote a letter to the regional leaders which was preserved through the writings of church historian Eusebius. In his letter, Constantine wrote:

> She [Eutropia] assures me, then, that the place which gains its name from the oak of Mambre [Mamre], where we find that Abraham dwelt is defiled by certain of the slaves of superstition in every possible way. She declares that idols which should be utterly destroyed have been erected on the site of that tree; that an altar is near the spot; and that impure sacrifices are continually performed.[11]

These impure sacrifices, observed and reported by Eutropia, demonstrate that at some point after Herod the Great enclosed the commemorative altar, pagans began sacrificing on it. Mader's team found several pieces of broken idols and a stone carving of Hermes.[12] In Greek mythology, Hermes was the messenger of the gods. That Hermes would have been worshiped at Mamre between the reigns of Herod and Constantine makes sense, because from the perspective of the pagan mind, the messenger who appeared to Abraham at Mamre would have been understood to be the Greek god Hermes.

Constantine issued orders to put an end to the pagan worship by burning the idols and to cleanse the site by building a church:

> That every idol which shall be found in the place above-mentioned shall immediately be consigned to the flames; that the altar be utterly demolished . . . the place itself we have directed to be adorned with an unpolluted structure . . . a church; in order that it may become a fitting place of assembly for holy men.[13]

In correlation with these historical sources, Mader uncovered the foundations of the church that was built to carry out Constantine's orders.

Img. 23: This picture shows the foundations of Constantine's church which Mader unearthed at Mamre.

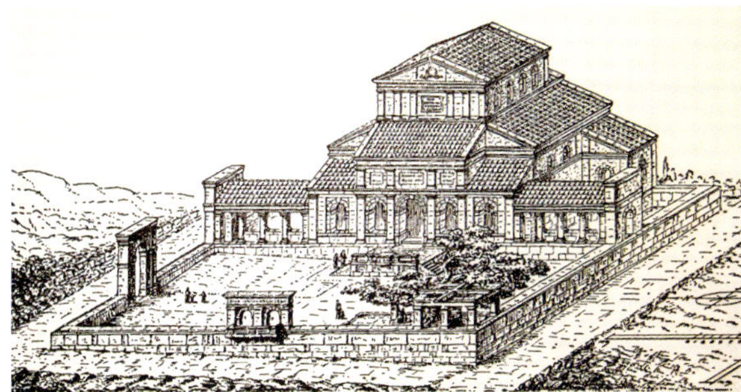

Img. 24: A reconstruction of Constantine's church at Mamre, from Mader's excavation report.

During his reign, Constantine commissioned only four churches in the Holy Land. That one of these was at Mamre shows how important the site was to Christianity. Of the four Constantinian churches that can currently be visited in Israel, the foundations and apse of the church at Mamre are the best preserved. However, compared to the other three, the construction of the church at Mamre was unusually wide and not very deep. Mader's explanation for this was that the church had been built between two pre-existing features which determined its unique dimensions: Herod's enclosure wall on the east and the site of Abraham's altar on the west.[14]

Img. 25: The reasons for the dimensions of Constantine's church at Mamre (red) are the two pre-existing structures: Herod's enclosure wall (green) and the altar (purple).

Layer 5

ISLAMIC PERIOD (After the Seventh Century AD)

Above the church's ruins, Mader found broken, scattered walls from the Islamic Period, which began when Muslims conquered the area in AD 638. The Islamic walls preserved the site and continued to mark its location. Since Abraham is venerated in Islam, the Muslims continued to commemorate his campsite at Mamre. Their recognition of Mamre as a sacred site explains why the Palestinian city of Hebron grew and expanded around Mamre rather than over the top of it.

WHY THE ARCHAEOLOGY MATTERS

The field of biblical archaeology has changed since the 1920s when Mader excavated Mamre. Today, biblical archaeology is dominated by secular scholars who generally do not believe in God, miracles, or the supernatural. Their naturalist views cause them to see the Bible as nothing but a myth.

For example, the well-known Israeli archaeologist Israel Finkelstein made the following stateWment in his popular book entitled *The Bible Unearthed*:

> Its [archaeology's] finds have revolutionized the study of early Israel and have cast serious doubt on the historical basis of such famous biblical stories as the wanderings of the patriarchs.... Some of the most famous events in the Bible clearly never happened at all.[15]

What Mader unearthed at Mamre becomes critical to refute this kind of argument against the Bible. According to Finkelstein and many of his like-minded colleagues, the events at Mamre never happened. Rather, these individuals consider the patriarchs to be made-up characters whose stories were composed much later in Israel's history. The evidence Mader uncovered easily refutes this, however, demonstrating that the site was already venerated long before the patriarchal "story" was supposedly authored. The stack of archaeological layers at Mamre stands as evidence for the historicity of the accounts recorded in the Bible.

To describe this in terms of our jigsaw puzzle example, imagine someone looking at the box cover of a puzzle and then declaring that, while the picture is nice, there never was an actual puzzle in the box. If, however, five puzzle pieces are dug up that match the picture on the box cover, it is no longer possible to say that the puzzle itself never existed. While artifacts alone can't be properly understood without the context of an ancient text, they do fully establish the actual, physical existence of what the text describes, demonstrating the text to be an accurate, historical record of real places, events, and people.

Since the archaeological evidence uncovered thus far demonstrates the Bible to be historically reliable, let us dig deeper to search out its spiritual significance.

THE INTERPRETATION

Around AD 130, a local Christian convert from paganism named Justin Martyr used the Hebrew Bible (Old Testament) to argue that Jesus was the Messiah. One of the evidences he offered in his attempt to persuade his listeners was the event that occurred at Mamre:

> Moses, then, that blessed and faithful servant of God, tells us that He who appeared to Abraham under the oak tree of Mamre was God, sent, with two accompanying angels.[16]

Justin merely pointed out what Jews already believed—that Moses was inspired by God when he wrote, "The Lord [Yahweh] appeared to Abraham near the great trees of Mamre" (Genesis 18:1). Justin went on to distinguish that it was Jesus who appeared at Mamre, not as God the Father but rather as preincarnate God the Son.

Declaring the same theology, Eusebius wrote about his visit to Mamre around AD 318:

> And he [Jesus] is no angel . . . but One greater than an angel, the God and Lord who was seen beside the before-mentioned oak with the two angels in human form . . . This would be our Lord and Savior . . . putting on a human form and shape, and revealed to the godly ancestor Abraham Who He was.[17]

As stated earlier, Constantine commissioned only four churches to be built in the Holy Land. Three of these churches were erected at locations where the New Testament records major events taking place in Jesus' life. Because of the Christian belief that it was actually Jesus who had appeared to Abraham, Constantine's church at Mamre is the only one to honor an event from the Old Testament.

According to Justin and Eusebius, the preincarnate Jesus had appeared to Abraham and Sarah at Mamre. Jesus came to them, promising that in the future He would, through their offspring, bless all the nations of earth. Jesus gave the promise. Jesus was the promise.

The evidence that He fulfilled His promise is seen in Mamre's archaeological record. Abraham built an altar (purple/layer 1) and worshiped the Lord for His promise of a son. The promised son was born and did indeed grow to be a people, eventually becoming the nation and Kingdom of Israel (blue/layer 2). From the line of those kings, a child was born in the time of Herod the Great (green/layer 3).

Herod tried to kill this child, while at the same time he was unknowingly building walls around the very place where this child had been promised. This child—Jesus—did come as promised. He lived, died, and then rose again to rescue mankind from sin, establishing a new covenant between God and man.

Now people from all nations, not just Israel, had a way to be in a righteous relationship with God. Through the centuries, Christian pilgrims from the nations, those blessed by the One promised to Abraham, traveled to Mamre (red/layer 4) to worship Him.

Mamre has been, and still is, a place to remember and worship the One promising and the One promised—Jesus, son of Abraham, Son of God, blessing to all the world.

NOTES

1. Yitzhak Magen, "Mamre. A Cultic Site from the Reign of Herod," in One Land–Many Cultures: Archaeological Studies in Honour of Stanislao Loffreda OFM, ed. G. Claudio Bottini, Leah Di Segni and L. Daniel Chrupcala (Jerusalem: Franciscan Printing Press, 2003), p. 245. Magen's note #3 on page 257 identifies him as the 1984-1986 excavation director.

2. Evaristus Mader, Mambre: Die Ergebnisse Der Ausgrabungen Im Heiligen Bezirk Ramet El-Halil In SudPalastina 1926–1928 (Freiburg im Breisgau: Erich Wewel Verlag, 1957), 48.

3. Ibid., drawing #37.

4. Ibid.

5. Ibid., 49. See also Joan E. Taylor, Christians and the Holy Places: The Myth of Jewish-Christian Origins (Oxford: Clarendon Press, 1993), 92; and Charles F. Pfeiffer, Wycliffe Dictionary of Biblical Archaeology (Peabody, MA: Hendrickson Publishers, 2000), 362.

6. There is a disagreement among scholars regarding when Abraham lived. The debate ranges between the twenty-first and nineteenth centuries BC. The evidence from Mamre establishes that the site was occupied throughout this range of dates, so for the purposes of this book, I have chosen the generalized and easy-to-remember, rounded-off date of 2000 BC.

7. Mader, Mambre: Die Ergebnisse Der Ausgrabungen, 48. See also drawing #37.

8. The two archaeologists who excavated Mamre, E. Mader in 1926–1928 and later Y. Magen in 1984–1986, identified Herod the Great as the builder of the monumental walls enclosing the site because the masonry style used at Mamre parallels other known Herodian sites (to be discussed later) and the pottery and other finds associated with these walls date to Herod's time.

9. Mader, Mambre: Die Ergebnisse Der Ausgrabungen, 25.

10. Magen, "Mamre. A Cultic Site," fig. 14, 253.

11. Eusebius, The Life of the Blessed Emperor Constantine, (London: Samuel Bagster and Sons, 1845), 156.

12. Mader, Mambre: Die Ergebnisse Der Ausgrabungen, plate 73, photograph 137, 135.

13. Eusebius, The Life of the Blessed Emperor Constantine, 156-57.

14. J. W. Crowfoot, Early Churches in Palestine, The Schweich Lectures on Biblical Archaeology (London: Published for the British Academy by H. Milford, Oxford University Press, 1941), 35.

15. Israel Finkelstein and Neil Asher Silberman, The Bible Unearthed (New York: Touchstone, 2002), 3, 5.

16. Justin Martyr, "Dialogue of Justin with Trypho, a Jew," in The Apostolic Fathers with Justin Martyr and Irenaeus, eds. Alexander Roberts, James Donaldson, and A. Cleveland Coxe, vol. 1, of The Ante-Nicene Fathers. (Buffalo, NY: The Christian Literature Company, 1885), 223.

17. Eusebius, The Proof of the Gospel: Being the Demonstratio Evangelica of Eusebius of Caesarea, ed. W. J. Sparrow-Simpson and W. K. L. Clarke, trans. William John Ferrar, vol. 1, Translations of Christian Literature: Series I: Greek Texts (London; New York: Society for Promoting Christian Knowledge; The Macmillan Company, 1920), 253–54.

In Jerusalem there is a holy place called Mount Moriah, very similar to Mamre, with one thing built on top of another. Like Mamre, Mount Moriah is also enclosed by walls built by Herod the Great.

Chapter 2
THE MOUNTAIN OF GOD

Mount Moriah is a holy place in Jerusalem similar to Mamre, except Mount Moriah has never been excavated. However, the events that took place there can be examined by studying about Mount Moriah in Scripture and in other historical texts. Additionally, various archaeological features and related evidences for this site are visible even without excavating.

What we'll see in the texts and the archaeology are two altars, two temples, two destructions, and two shrines. The altars were built by Abraham and David. The temples were built by Solomon and Zerubbabel but destroyed during the reigns of Nebuchadnezzar and Vespasian. The shrines that followed were built by Hadrian and Abd al-Malik.

After examining all these events, we'll look at the promise to Abraham and see his descendants' connection to those altars, temples, destructions, and shrines.

THE REGION OF MORIAH

After the Lord fulfilled His promise to give Abraham and Sarah a son, He appeared to Abraham once again and said,

> "Take your son, your only son, whom you love—Isaac—and go to the region of Moriah. Sacrifice him there as a burnt offering on a mountain I will show you." ... On the third day Abraham looked up and saw the place in the distance. (Genesis 22:2, 4)

God instructed Abraham to sacrifice his promised son "on a mountain" in "the region of Moriah." Before we examine the events that occurred there, it is important to identify where the "region" of Moriah is located.

The region of Moriah (see *Img. 26*) is located between two major ridges: one ridge on the west (marked Watershed Ridge on the topography) and another to the east called the Mount of Olives. Between these two ridges, "the region of Moriah" is made up of three major valleys that define two hills. Moving from west to east, the three valleys are Ben Hinnom, Central, and Kidron. The Ben Hinnom Valley makes up the region's western border, then swings around to form its southern border, while the Kidron Valley forms the region's eastern border. In the middle, the Central Valley divides two hills: the Western Hill and the Eastern Hill. Located on the lowest and southern-most portion of the Eastern Hill is the Gihon Spring, which is the region's main water source. At the time of Abraham, the city of Salem was located near this spring. To the north of the city of Salem is the uppermost part of the Eastern Hill. The top of the Eastern Hill, which peaks in a rocky outcropping, is Mount Moriah, where the Lord directed Abraham to sacrifice Isaac.

ABRAHAM'S ALTAR (c. 2000 BC)

The Genesis account tells us that Abraham built an altar on top of Mount Moriah.

> Abraham took the wood for the burnt offering and placed it on his son Isaac, and he himself carried the fire and the knife. As the two of them went on together, Isaac spoke up and said to his father Abraham, "Father?" "Yes, my son?" Abraham replied. "The fire and wood are here," Isaac said, "but where is the lamb for the burnt offering?" Abraham answered, "God himself will provide the lamb for the burnt offering, my son." And the two of them went on together. When they reached the place God had told him about, Abraham built

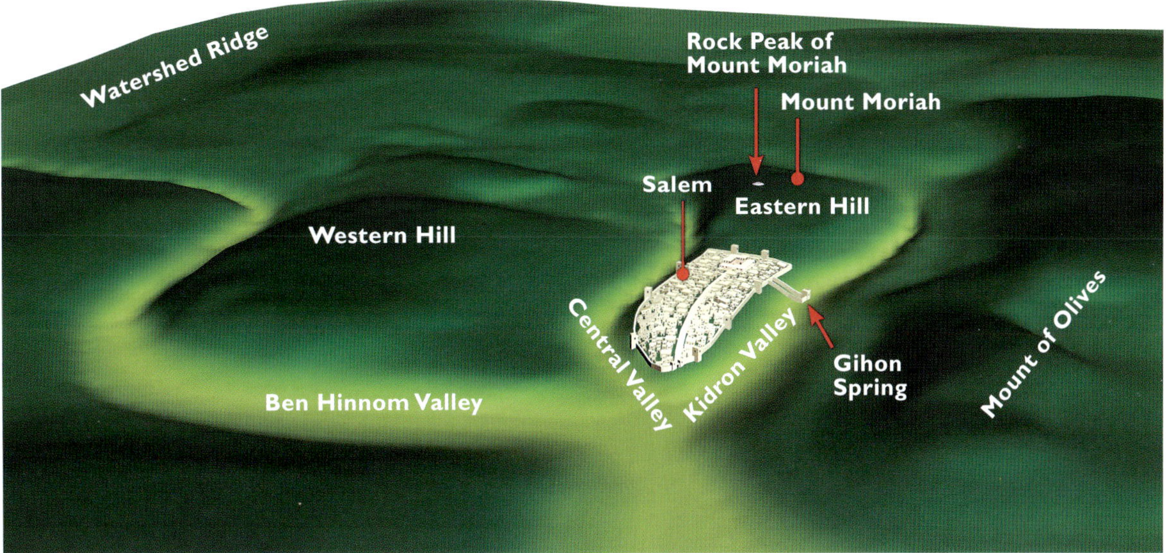

Img. 26: The topography of the region of Moriah at the time of Abraham, including the city of Salem, which would become Jerusalem.

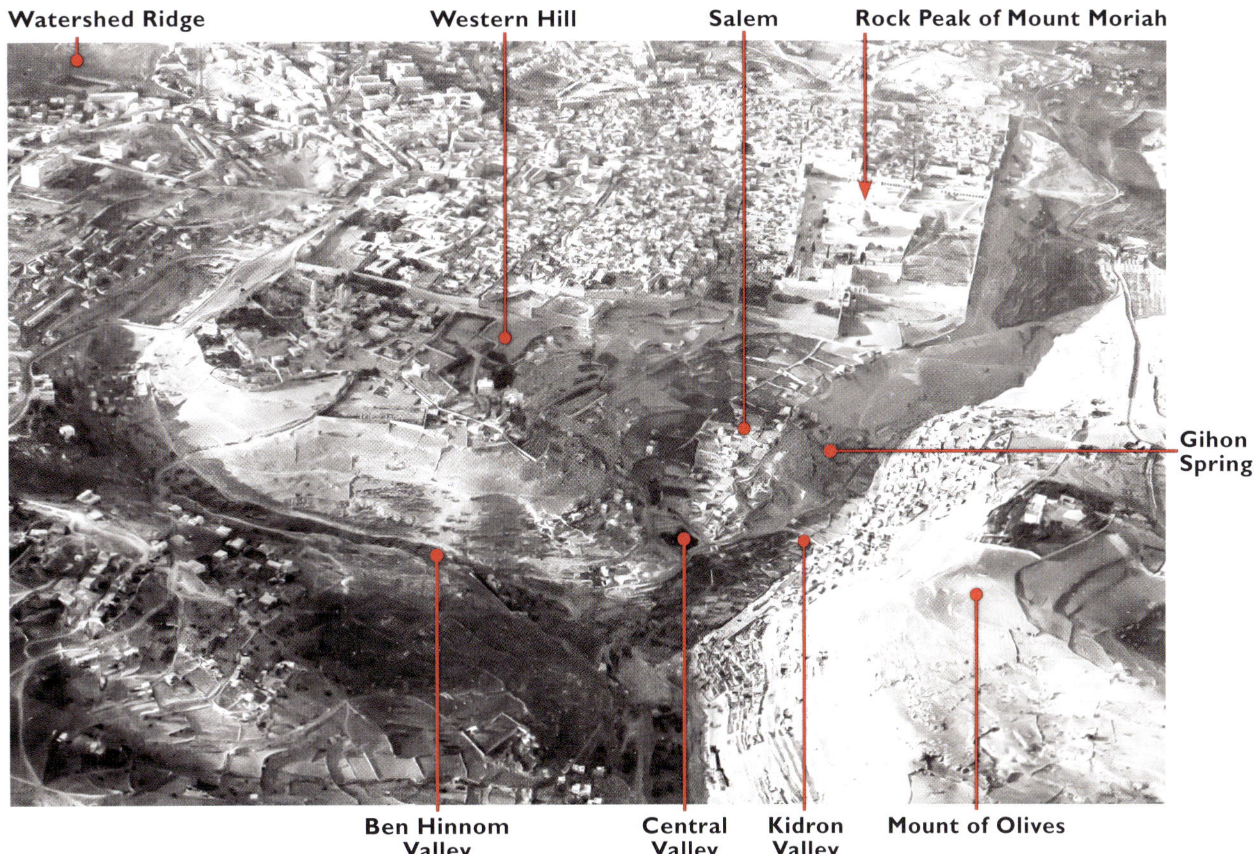

Img. 27: Aerial photo of Jerusalem (1931), showing the same geographical features as Img. 26. The Central Valley was deeper in ancient times. Now it has been filled in to flatten the topography for building the city over the valley. Mount Moriah (as seen above) is covered by the Temple Mount, and the rock peak of Mount Moriah now lies under the Dome of the Rock.

> an altar there and arranged the wood on it. He bound his son Isaac and laid him on the altar, on top of the wood. Then he reached out his hand and took the knife to slay his son. But the angel of the Lord called out to him from heaven, "Abraham! Abraham!" "Here I am," he replied. "Do not lay a hand on the boy," he said. "Do not do anything to him. Now I know that you fear God, because you have not withheld from me your son, your only son." Abraham looked up and there in a thicket he saw a ram caught by its horns. He went over and took the ram and sacrificed it as a burnt offering instead of his son. So Abraham called the place The Lord Will Provide. And to this day it is said, "On the mountain of the Lord it will be provided." The angel of the Lord called to Abraham from heaven a second time and said, "I swear by myself, declares the Lord, that because you have done this and have not withheld your son, your only son, I will surely bless you and make your descendants as numerous as the stars in the sky and as the sand on the seashore. Your descendants will take possession of the cities of their enemies, and through your offspring all nations on earth will be blessed, because you have obeyed me."(Genesis 22:6-18)

Abraham obeyed God. He built an altar, laid his son on it, and "took the knife"—but the LORD saved Isaac's life. He provided an animal to die in Isaac's place, and this event would later help all of Israel to understand the sacrificial system established through the Law given to Moses. A substitute would pay the death-price of sin:

> For the life of a creature is in the blood, and I have given it to you to make atonement for yourselves on the altar; it is the blood that makes atonement for one's life. (Leviticus 17:11)

DAVID'S ALTAR (Tenth Century BC)

The next layer to examine as we unearth the holy place of Moriah in Scripture is in a story about King David. At one point during his reign, David took a census to count the number of fighting men in his army. Long before Israel became a kingdom, during the time of the Exodus, God gave specific instructions about census taking. God's law stated that each person "must pay the LORD a ransom for his life" at the time he or she was counted, or a plague would break out on the people (Exodus 30:12). Unfortunately, David trusted in the size of his army rather than in the LORD and broke the commands regarding how a census was to be taken. We read the consequences here:

> So the LORD sent a plague on Israel from that morning until the end of the time designated, and seventy-thousand of the people from Dan to Beersheba died. . . . the angel of the LORD was then at the threshing floor of Araunah the Jebusite. When David saw the angel who was striking down the people, he said to the LORD, "I have sinned; I, the shepherd, have done wrong." . . . On that day Gad went to David and said to him, "Go up and build an altar to the LORD on the threshing floor of Araunah the Jebusite." So David went up, as the LORD had commanded through Gad. . . . So David bought the threshing floor and the oxen and paid fifty shekels of silver for them. David built an altar to the LORD there and sacrificed burnt offerings and fellowship offerings. Then the LORD answered his prayer in behalf of the land, and the plague on Israel was stopped. (2 Samuel 24:15, 16-19, 24-25)

David had sinned, and his people were paying the price. Again, God provided a way of rescue through an altar—an altar built on a threshing floor.

A threshing floor (see *Img. 28*) was a place to separate grain from chaff (grain's inedible outer covering). To thresh grain, an animal, usually an ox, pulled a wooden threshing sled over the stocks of barley or wheat. This cracked the husk, breaking it off of the grain. After the grain was threshed, winnowing forks were used to throw the smashed piles up into the air. This was often done on hilltops because they were open to wind. Up in the air, the lightweight chaff blew away, while the heavier grain fell back to the ground.

The grain was then collected and stored to be made into bread, while the worthless chaff was gathered into piles and burned.

When the LORD commanded David to build his altar on a threshing floor, it was so that he could separate David from his sin. The blood of the sacrificed oxen paid the penalty for David so that the LORD could forgive him. Sin was destroyed, not the sinner. The plague was stopped.

Neither Abraham nor David chose the location for their altars. The LORD directed them.

To Abraham he said,

> "Take your son, your only son, whom you love—Isaac—and go to the region of Moriah. Sacrifice him there as a burnt offering on a mountain I will show you." (Genesis 22:2)

And to David,

> On that day Gad went to David and said to him, "Go up and build an altar to the LORD on the threshing floor of Araunah the Jebusite." So David went up, as the LORD had commanded through Gad. . . . So David bought the threshing floor. (2 Samuel 24:18-19, 24)

God's instructions to Abraham and David were purposeful. He was directing them to the same place. David's threshing-floor altar was on top of Mount Moriah, where Abraham's altar had held Isaac centuries before. We know this because God directed one more altar be built at this same place on Mount Moriah—the altar of His temple.

SOLOMON'S TEMPLE (967 BC)

In 2 Chronicles 3:1 we read,

> Then Solomon began to build the temple of the LORD in Jerusalem on Mount Moriah [Abraham's altar], where the LORD had appeared to his father David. It was on the threshing floor of Araunah the Jebusite [David's altar], the place provided by David.

David provided Solomon with the place to build a temple for the LORD. But God had chosen that location long before it belonged to David and had been building layer upon

Img. 28: Men winnowing at a threshing floor (1940).

Img. 29: The Lord instructed both Abraham and David to build an altar and to sacrifice on Mount Moriah.

layer of sacrifice and atonement through the lives of Abraham, David, and now Solomon.

Solomon's temple had an altar of sacrifice. It was an altar for all the people of Israel. What Abraham, Isaac, and David had needed individually, Israel needed corporately—forgiveness. What God had provided for Abraham, Isaac, and David individually, He provided for Israel collectively—substitute sacrifice. Because the people of Israel knew their sinfulness, they brought sacrifices to the temple as God had instructed them to do. God accepted those substitute animals and forgave Israel's sin.

> Solomon offered a sacrifice of fellowship offerings to the Lord: twenty-two thousand cattle and a hundred and twenty thousand sheep and goats. So the king and all the Israelites dedicated the temple of the Lord. (1 Kings 8:63)
>
> Then the temple of the Lord was filled with the cloud, and the priests could not perform their service because of the cloud, for the glory of the Lord filled the temple of God. (2 Chronicles 5:13-14)

From all the world's countless hills, Yahweh, the God of Israel, chose this hill of Moriah to be the place where He received sacrifices, forgave sin, and dwelled with His people.

BABYLONIAN DESTRUCTION (586 BC)

Despite the provision of the temple's sacrificial system, Israel forsook their God and instead worshiped the false gods of the surrounding nations. They neither obeyed God's law nor sought His forgiveness. Therefore, in 586 BC the army of the Babylonian king Nebuchadnezzar destroyed Jerusalem and her temple. "He set fire to the temple of the Lord, the royal palace and all the houses of Jerusalem. Every important building he burned down" (2 Kings 25:9).

ZERUBBABEL'S TEMPLE (516 BC)

As we continue to move through the textual layers, we read in the Bible that the temple was rebuilt on its original site by Zerubbabel in the Persian Period:

> In the first year of King Cyrus, the king issued a decree concerning the temple of God in Jerusalem: Let the temple be rebuilt as a place to present sacrifices....

Img. 30: Solomon built the temple on Mount Moriah with an altar of sacrifice in front of its entrance.

> Let the governor of the Jews [Zerubbabel] and the Jewish elders rebuild this house of God on its site. (Ezra 6:3, 7)

Zerubbabel's temple was built "on its site," meaning on its original site: "He [Cyrus] has granted us new life to rebuild the house of our God and repair its ruins" (Ezra 9:9).

The second temple was built on top of the burned ruins of the first temple. The textual layers are stacking up: two altars (Abraham and David), one temple (Solomon), one destruction (Babylon), another temple (Zerubbabel) . . . and one destruction to come.

HEROD'S TEMPLE (First Century BC)

In the Early Roman Period, Herod the Great served as the king of Judea under the authority of the Roman emperor, Augustus Caesar. Josephus, the first century Jewish and Roman historian, described Herod's most monumental building project:

> In the eighteenth year of his reign, Herod started to enlarge and reconstruct the temple at his own expense, which he knew would be his greatest enterprise. . . . The temple itself was built by the priests in a year and a half, and was dedicated in a great celebration.[1]

Herod did not move Zerubbabel's temple, but rather he enlarged and glorified it on its original site.

ROMAN DESTRUCTION (AD 70)

Herod's temple was glorious to look upon; however, in Matthew 24:1-2 Jesus prophesied that it would be destroyed.

> Jesus left the temple and was walking away when his disciples came up to him to call his attention to its buildings. "Do you see all these things?" he asked. "Truly I tell you, not one stone here will be left on another; every one will be thrown down."

Notice Jesus is not referring to the Temple Mount, the massive, walled-in foundation that the temple was built on, but rather to the buildings which were sitting on top of that foundation.

Jesus' words were fulfilled in AD 70 by the Roman emperor Vespasian. He ordered Jerusalem's

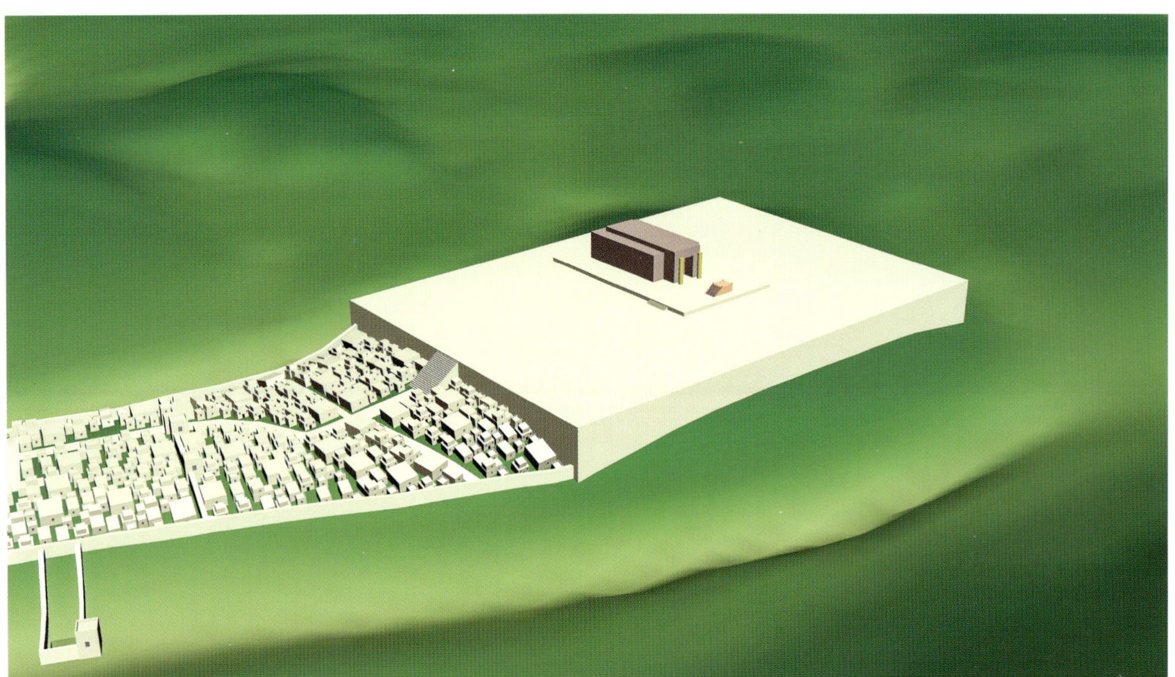

Img. 31: Zerubbabel's temple.

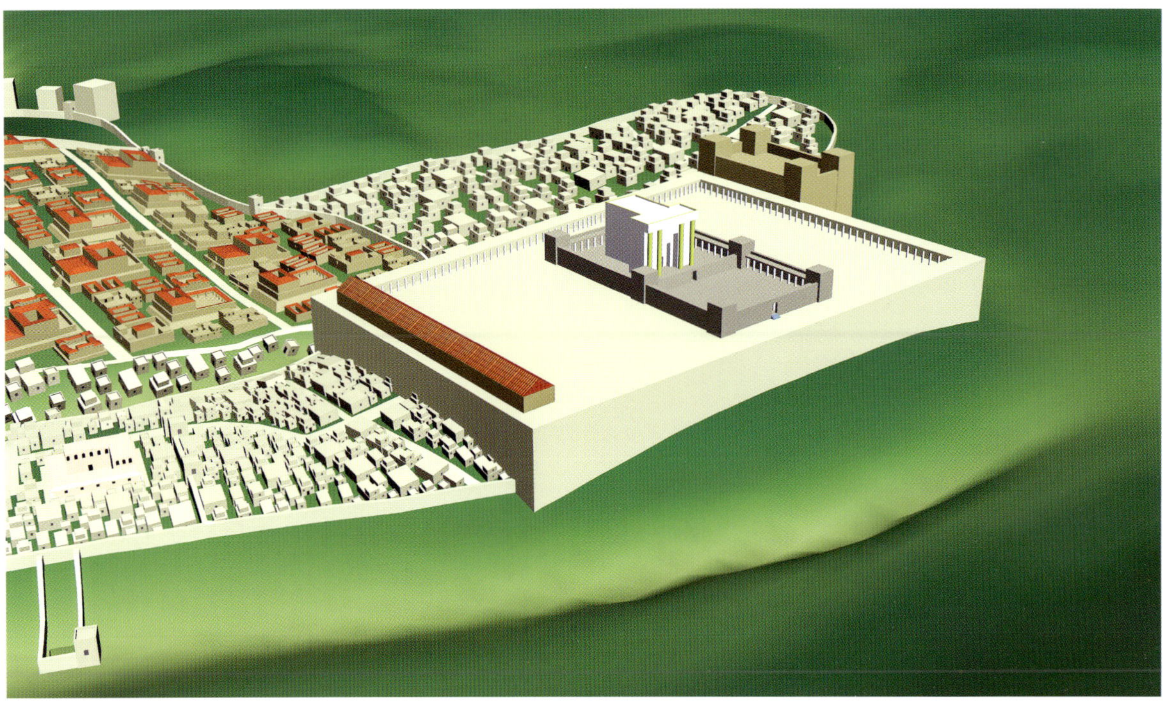

Img. 32: Herod the Great's temple.

Img. 33: The top of Mount Moriah is adorned with statues of Hadrian and Jupiter.

destruction, which was carried out by his son Titus. Again, we have Josephus describing the scene as an eyewitness:

> Around the altar were heaps of corpses, while streams of blood flowed down the steps of the sanctuary ... the Romans pitched their standards [of their gods] inside the temple court and offered sacrifice ... Caesar ordered the entire city and temple smashed to the ground.[2]

The Jewish Temple was completely destroyed. It lay in ruins, no stone upon another, all of them having been "thrown down" off the Temple Mount platform upon which the Temple had stood.

HADRIAN'S SHRINE (AD 130)

Approximately sixty years after the Temple was burned to the ground, Roman emperor Hadrian visited the ruins of Jerusalem and decided to build a new pagan city over the rubble of the former Jewish city. This led to a Jewish uprising known in history as the Bar Kokhba revolt. Dio Cassius, a Roman historian, recorded Hadrian's plan for the top of Jerusalem's holy hill:

> But [Hadrian] stirred up a war of no small extent or duration by founding a city at Jerusalem in place of that which had been destroyed, which city he named Aelia Capitolina, and by setting up another temple to Jupiter on the site of the Lord's Temple.[3]

While Cassius tells of Hadrian's plan to build a temple, it seems that what he actually built was possibly smaller in nature, more like a shrine. This shrine seems to have still been partially intact in the fourth century AD when Jerome, one of the influential figures of the early church, visited the Temple Mount. He described what he observed on the Temple Mount: "Where once were the temple and the religion of God, there a statue of Hadrian and an idol of Jupiter are set up together."[4]

Img. 34: Bust of Hadrian

These two images standing next to each other represented the Roman worldview of the close relationship between the earthly and heavenly kings. Romans believed Jupiter was king of the gods and their emperor was king of earth. What had once been the very dwelling place of Yahweh was now desecrated. People worshiped the Imperial Cult, while looking to these two towering pillars on top of Mount Moriah as their gods.

BYZANTINE PERIOD (AD 324–638)

Sometime after Jerome's visit, during the Christian Byzantine Period, Hadrian's shrine was removed, and the foundation where the Jewish Temple had stood lay empty. We know this from pilgrim accounts that describe the Temple Mount in their day as barren, without any buildings.

ISLAMIC SHRINE (AD 692 to Present)

The Temple Mount remained desolate until Byzantine-controlled Jerusalem was surrendered to Caliph Omar (also spelled Umar) in AD 638. Following the surrender, Omar was shown the city's famous Jewish holy place. Here is an account of this event:

> Then Umar said to him [Sophronius, Byzantine bishop of Jerusalem]: "You owe me a rightful debt. Give me a place in which I might build a sanctuary." The patriarch said to him. . . . "It is the rock. . . . It is in the center of the world and was a Temple for the Israelites, who held it in great veneration and wherever they were they turned their faces toward it during prayer." . . . The Byzantines, however, neglected it and did not hold it in veneration, nor did they build a church over it because Christ our Lord said in his Holy Gospel, "Not a stone will be left upon a stone which will not be ruined and devastated." For this reason the Christians left it as a ruin and did not build a church over it.[5]

Img. 35: Model of Byzantine Jerusalem on display on the church property of Saint Peter in Gallicantu. Notice the barren Temple Mount in the background with nothing built on it.

Img. 36: The Temple Mount during the Byzantine Period.

"The rock" shown to Omar was the rocky top of Mount Moriah over which the Holy of Holies of the Temple had stood. This source also explains why no church was ever built on the Temple Mount during the Byzantine Period: to honor Jesus' prophecy of no stones being left on another.

Omar had the area cleaned, but his vision of building a sanctuary was actually completed by a later Caliph named Abd al-Malik. In AD 692, Caliph Abd al-Malik finished the Islamic shrine, today called the Dome of the Rock. So, understandably, it is not possible to excavate Mount Moriah. However, the archaeology is visible—if one looks carefully.

THE ARCHAEOLOGY

Even without excavations, plenty of evidence exists to identify and verify the Temple Mount as the authentic location of Mount Moriah. In addition, there is direct archaeological evidence found at sites near to and abutting the Temple Mount, which also helps to trace its history and clarify our understanding of the site.

Let's work our way back through time to consider what was left behind from the periods and events discussed in the first section.

DOME OF THE ROCK (AD 692 to Present)

Though it has been remodeled many times, the Dome of the Rock has marked Jerusalem's most venerated spot for more than thirteen hundred years. The sacred peak of Mount Moriah is the rock which gives The Dome of the Rock its name. This rock is the oldest physical evidence for Jerusalem's holy hill.

LAYER 8
Islamic Shrine

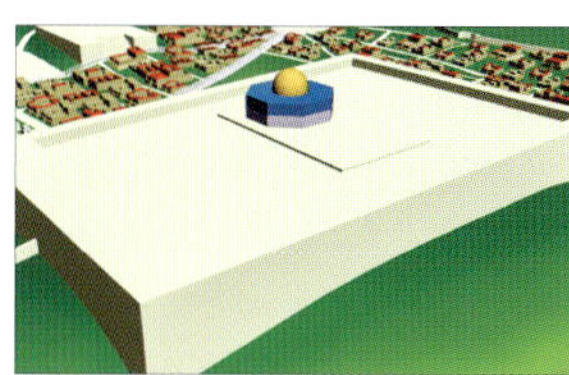

LAYER 7
Barren Temple Mount

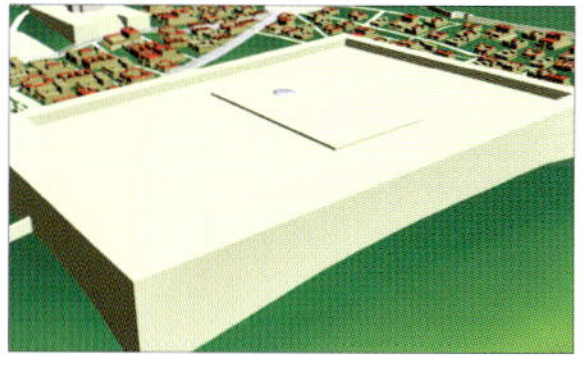

LAYER 6
Hadrian's Shrine

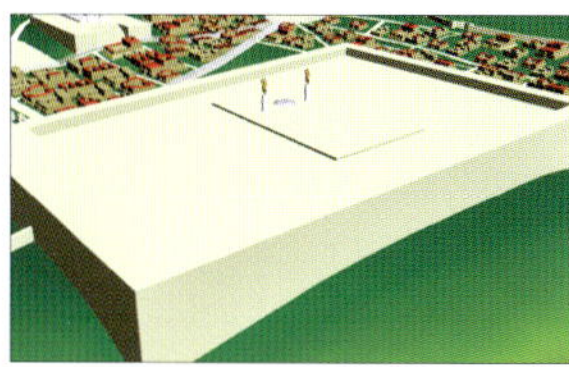

LAYER 5
Herod's Temple

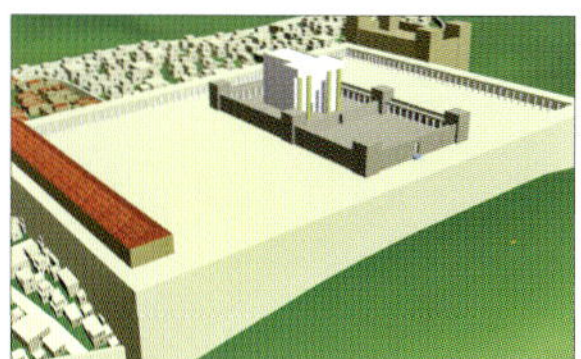

LAYER 4
Zerubbabel's Temple

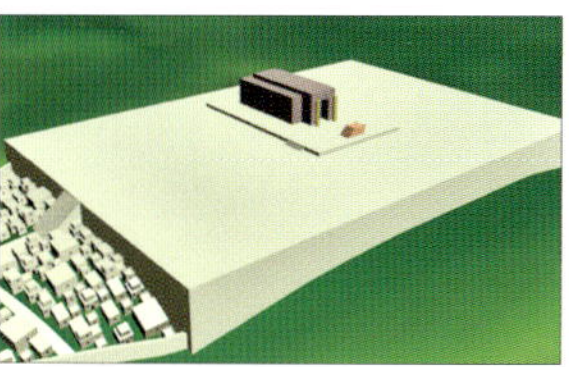

LAYER 3
Solomon's Temple

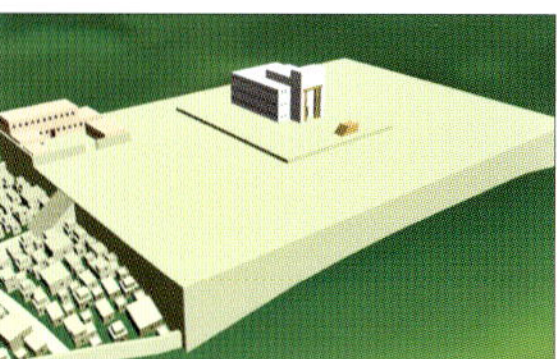

LAYER 2
David's Altar

LAYER 1
Abraham's Altar

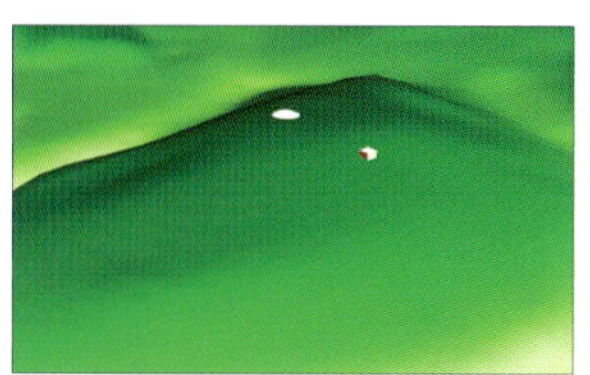

Img. 37: (column to the right) The major archaeological layers which the Bible describes show just how much Mount Moriah has changed over almost four thousand years of history. The column of images include: the two altars, the two temples, and the two shrines. Herod expanded the second temple, and the Byzantines left the Temple Mount bare.

Img. 38: Remains of the Arch rebuilt by Hadrian.

Img. 39: This is the rock peak of Mount Moriah. It is this outcropping of rock which gives the name to the Islamic shrine, the Dome of the Rock.

Img. 40: The Dome of the Rock

HADRIAN'S SHRINE (AD 130)

The remains of arches dating to the time of Hadrian can be seen in the ceiling of an enclosed area, currently in use as a prayer hall, located just to the north of the Western Wall. These arches likely supported a road which led up to Hadrian's shrine on the Temple Mount.

ROMAN DESTRUCTION (AD 70)

The Roman destruction of Jerusalem in AD 70 left the Temple Mount ruined. A pile of massive stones uncovered during the excavations of Benjamin Mazar (1968–1982) attest to the utter decimation that occurred. Israeli archaeologist Hillel Geva, one of the dig's participants, described the discovery:

> We have vivid, concrete evidence for the violent conquest of Jerusalem by Roman Legions in 70 C.E. and the intensive destruction of its buildings. Deep accumulations of stones from the walls and buildings of the Temple Mount were encountered in B. Mazar's excavations next to the southern and western walls.[6]

These piles of massive stones, which Josephus describes as "smashed to ground," provide dramatic evidence of the fulfillment of Jesus' prediction that the magnificent buildings on the Temple Mount would be destroyed. Jesus said the stones would all be "thrown down" (Matthew 24:2, Mark 13:2), and they were. Roman soldiers rolled them to the edge of the Temple Mount platform and pushed them off onto the streets below.

HEROD'S TEMPLE (First Century BC)

Herod's Temple Mount, the colossal platform on which the temple stood, remains the dominating and defining ancient feature still visible in Jerusalem today. The enormous stones used to construct the Temple Mount's retaining walls continue to impress visitors. The west-facing retaining wall of the Temple Mount, called the Western Wall, is the most sacred Jewish holy place in Jerusalem. It is the closest place that Jews can gather to where their temple once stood.

Img. 41: A Jewish youth mourns among fallen stones on Tisha B'Av (the 9th day of the month of Av), which is the anniversary of the destruction of the Jewish temple.

Img. 42: These stones are from demolished buildings which were pushed over the edge of the Temple Mount's foundation walls in the AD 70 destruction of Jerusalem—leaving no stone upon another, just as Jesus had prophesied. They are still piled up where they fell.

Img. 43: Jews are gathered at the Western Wall to celebrate the Feast of Tabernacles. The Temple Mount walls, facing north, south, and west, were all constructed by Herod the Great when he expanded the Temple Mount platform. This is the most important Jewish holy site in the world, because it is the place closest to the Holy of Holies of the previous temple.

ZERUBBABEL'S TEMPLE (516 BC)

Toward the southern end of the east-facing wall of the Temple Mount is a seam that can be seen in the stone masonry (see *Img. 44*). This seam was created when Herod the Great enlarged the area by extending the walls towards the south. The construction to the left of the seam belongs to Herod's extension, making the masonry to the right of the seam older. Kathleen Kenyon, one of Jerusalem's excavators, explains,

> The surviving masonry, to the right of the straight joint . . . is likely to be in origin that of Zerubbabel, though an analysis of the courses visible suggests that there may be about three styles possibly representing rebuilds during the stormy life of Zerubbabel's Temple.[7]

This seam is observable evidence which points to the existence of Zerubbabel's Temple.

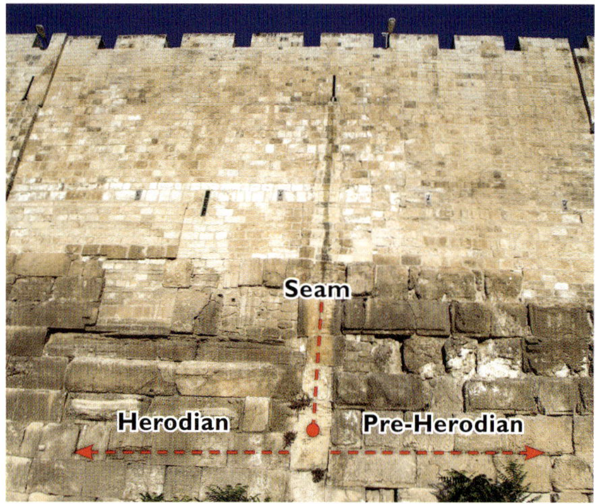

Img. 44: Seam on the Temple Mount.

BABYLONIAN DESTRUCTION (586 BC)

The Temple Mount would have to be excavated in order to find the Babylonian burn-destruction layer. However, we must keep in mind that the temple area was only part of the overall city of Jerusalem at that time. While the Temple Mount itself remains unexcavated, Jerusalem has been dug extensively, and the evidence for the Babylonian destruction of Jerusalem is abundant.

Img. 45: Walls uncovered from the Babylonian destruction layer in Jerusalem.

Consider the description of Yigal Shiloh's excavations:

> The massive destruction of Jerusalem by the Babylonians is apparent not only in the thick layers of charred remains unearthed in structures such as the Burnt Room and the Bullae House, but also in the deep stone rubble from collapsed buildings found covering the eastern slope.[8]

SOLOMON'S TEMPLE (967 BC)

Just as the remains of an Israelite gate were found outside Herod's enclosure walls at Mamre, so too, in Jerusalem, a portion of Solomon's walls were found just south of Herod's Temple Mount. The archaeologist Eilat Mazar described the discovery in her book, *Discovering the Solomonic Wall in Jerusalem*:

> In the process of excavating through the later layers . . . we not only discovered well-preserved First Temple period walls, but also intact floor layers with *in-situ* pottery vessels. . . . Dating the construction of the fortification line in the Ophel to sometime in the second half of the 10th century makes King Solomon out to be the best candidate for its architect.[9]

While Solomon's temple can't be explored archaeologically, the walls he built to enclose the temple within the greater area of Jerusalem, written of in 1 Kings 9:15, have been found.

DAVID'S ALTAR

The Jebusite city that David conquered and established as his capital has come to be called the City of David. It is one of the most excavated ancient cities in the world, and the evidence for it's occupation at the time of King David is certain. We will cover important archaeological discoveries relating to David and his city in chapter 5. But as it relates to this chapter, understand that the nearest high place to the City of David was Mount Moriah. The ancients most often performed their rites of worship on high places, so it would have made sense to David to be directed by God to the nearest high place to build his altar, offer sacrifices, and worship Yahweh there.

Img. 46: The walls of a monumental building, dating to the reign of King David, discovered by Dr. Eilat Mazar in the City of David.

Img. 47: A section of the Solomonic wall between the City of David and the Temple Mount, excavated by Eilat Mazar. Solomon built these walls to extend the city to the north, thereby incorporating the temple, which he had built on Moriah, into the city of Jerusalem.

Img. 48: The monumental building walls.

Img. 49: Original steps to Herod's temple.

Img. 50: An aerial view of the City of David (left center) and the southern side of the Temple Mount (right center).

Img. 51: Solomonic walls.

Img. 52: Seam in the masonry.

Img. 53: An inscription on the inside of the circular roof of the Dome of the Rock, dating to the shrine's construction in AD 692. A portion of this dedicatory inscription is also found in the Koran and reads, "So believe in God and all the messengers, and stop talking about a Trinity. . . . Say only the truth about Jesus over whom you dispute: he is the son of Mary! It is not fitting that God should beget or father a son."[10]

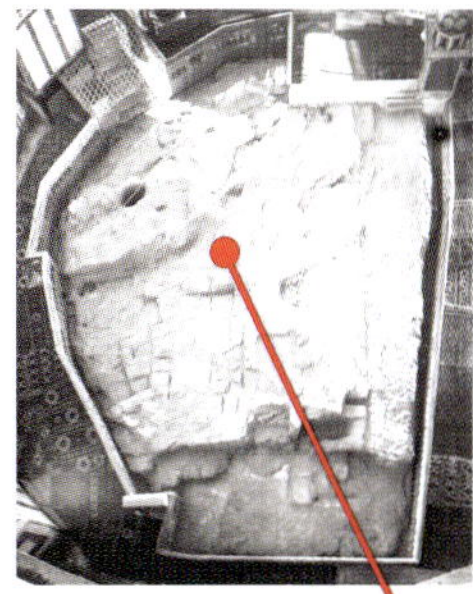

Img. 54: Mount Moriah's rocky peak.

Img. 55: Hadrian's Arch.

Img. 56: Temple Mount, looking east.

Img. 57: The Western Wall (west-facing wall of the Temple Mount).

Img. 58: Pile of massive stones from the AD 70 Roman destruction.

Img. 59: A Bedouin winnowing his grain, illustrating what John said about Jesus: "His winnowing fork is in his hand to clear his threshing floor and to gather the wheat into his barn, but he will burn up the chaff with unquenchable fire" (Luke 3:17).

ABRAHAM'S ALTAR

Once we work our way through all the layers, back to Abraham's altar, we find ourselves coming full circle back to the position of having to see through Scripture instead of through excavations. Because we can't dig this most sacred site, we don't know what might be unearthed that would relate to Abraham. Our limitation in excavating, however, does not hamper our ability to understand the power of what occurred at that place. When we think about the significance of what happened on Abraham's altar, we begin to realize that the significance of Mount Moriah isn't just in the place itself. The significance of Mount Moriah is a Person.

THE INTERPRETATION

To fully understand Mount Moriah's significance, we must understand how the place relates to the Person of Christ. Mark 15:37-39 tells us,

> With a loud cry, Jesus breathed his last. The curtain of the temple was torn in two from top to bottom. And when the centurion, who stood there in front of Jesus, saw how he died, he said, "Surely this man was the Son of God!"

Three things happened in these verses: Jesus died, the curtain was torn, and the centurion believed. Salvation had come to mankind. But how does this relate to Mount Moriah?

JESUS DIED

On Mount Moriah, Abraham "looked up and there in a thicket he saw a ram . . . and sacrificed it as a burnt offering instead of his son" (Genesis 22:13). Centuries later John the Baptist looked up and, seeing Jesus, cried out, "Look, the Lamb of God, who takes away the sin of the world!" (John 1:29).

As a perfect parallel to the story of Abraham and Isaac, our expectation might be that Jesus' sacrifice would have to take place on Mount Moriah. However, Scripture clearly tells us where Jesus breathed His last. "And so Jesus also suffered *outside the city* gate to make the people holy through his own blood" (Hebrews 13:12, emphasis added).

Jesus shed His blood outside the city, not at the temple on Mount Moriah. However, Jesus' death dramatically affected the most sacred place on Mount Moriah—the Holy of Holies in the temple.

THE CURTAIN WAS TORN

Immediately, as Jesus breathed His last breath, the curtain in front of the Holy of Holies ripped open from top to bottom. This curtain had always been the separating boundary between sinful, unholy people and a most holy God. Now, however, the curtain was ripped open and access to God was restored:

> We have been made holy through the sacrifice of the body of Jesus Christ once for all. For by one sacrifice he has made perfect forever those who are being made holy. Therefore, brothers and sisters, since we have confidence to enter the Most Holy Place by the blood of Jesus, by a new and living way opened for us through the curtain, that is, his body. (Hebrews 10:10, 14, 19-20)

THE CENTURION BELIEVED

As the curtain at the temple ripped, something amazing was happening at the cross. A Roman centurion (Mark 15:39) was experiencing the barrier between God and man being torn open. As he saw Jesus die, this soldier understood and believed "that Jesus was the Son of God"—a Son who was willing to open up a way to His holy Father in heaven by paying with His own life.

What the high priest had always done for the Jewish people each year on the Day of Atonement, Jesus had now accomplished for the Gentile centurion—He opened up a way to safely be in the presence of God. By believing, the centurion spiritually stepped through the torn curtain into relationship with God. From that day on, all people who understood that Jesus was God's son and believed that He had paid for their sin could approach God with confidence, because they were now covered with Christ's righteousness, not their own sin.

What the Old Covenant and the temple had only foreshadowed, Jesus had fulfilled: confidence to enter into the Most Holy Place, the ability to be intimately related to God. The new had come. The old was obsolete and would soon disappear (Hebrews 8:13). Within forty years of Christ's death, Herod's temple was razed to the ground, with no stone left upon another. It has never been rebuilt, and it is no longer needed. Atonement is no longer found in the temple atop Mount Moriah. Moriah's atonement is found in Jesus.

THE TEMPTATION

Before Jesus could offer Himself as our atonement, however, He had a spiritual test to undergo, similar to what Abraham had experienced many years before on Mount Moriah.

Shortly after Jesus began His ministry on earth, He was baptized and then led by the Holy Spirit to the Judean wilderness for forty days of fasting. During that time, Satan appeared to Jesus and attempted to engage Him in a series of temptations. In their final, climactic encounter, the devil led Jesus to the holy mountain where they stood on top of what Jesus called His "Father's house" (Luke 2:49 and John 2:16).

> The devil led him [Jesus] to Jerusalem and had him stand on the highest point of the temple. "If you are the Son of God," he said, "throw yourself down from here. For it is written: 'He will command his angels concerning you to guard you carefully; they will lift you up in their hands, so that you will not strike your foot against a stone.'" Jesus answered, "It is said, 'Do not put the Lord your God to the test.'" When the devil had finished all this tempting, he left him until an opportune time. (Luke 4:9-13)

"If you are the Son of God," was Satan's challenge to Jesus. To put it in other words, Satan's taunt was, "Prove who you are!" If Jesus had fallen for the temptation, He would have exalted Himself just as Hadrian later did when he raised his image up on a pedestal over that same spot. Instead, Jesus submitted Himself to His Father's will. He had already come down from heaven, and soon He would humble Himself even lower and die outside of the city.

Jesus won in that encounter with Satan. But the same challenge is still being spoken from the exact same place. Where the temple once stood, the Dome of the Rock now rises into the air, housing a dedicatory inscription that for more than thirteen centuries has declared that Jesus is not the Son of God. Over the very place where the devil said to Jesus, "If you are the Son of God," the inscription reads, "It is not fitting that God should beget or father a son."[11] These words betray the truth found in John 3:16, "For God so loved the world that he gave his one and only Son, that whoever believes in him shall not perish but have eternal life."

Satan lost his chance to ruin God's plan of redemption, but he has not stopped trying to tempt. Now his temptations are focused on every human soul. Every person must face the test of making a choice: self-exaltation and denial of God, or humility and acceptance of the need for Christ's sacrifice.

Hadrian failed the test. He used Mount Moriah to glorify himself. The centurion passed the test. Seeing Christ on the cross, he understood what the ripped curtain had unveiled and cried out, "Surely this man was the Son of God!"

NOTES

1. Flavius Josephus, Josephus: The Essential Writings, trans. and ed. Paul L. Maier (Grand Rapids, MI: Kregel Publications, 1988), 247.

2. Ibid., 360–61, 363, 369.

3. Dio Cassius, Roman History, quoted in F. E. Peters, Jerusalem: The Holy City in the Eyes of Chroniclers, Visitors, Pilgrims, and Prophets from the Days of Abraham to the Beginnings of Modern Times (Princeton, NJ: Princeton University Press, 1985), 126.

4. Jerome Commentary on Isaiah, quoted in Jack Finegan, The Archaeology of the New Testament: The Life of Jesus and the Beginning of the Early Church, Rev. ed. (Princeton, NJ: Princeton University Press, 1992), 199.

5. J. D. Baldi, Enchiridion Locorum Sanctorum (1955): 447–48, quoted in F. E. Peters, Jerusalem: The Holy City, 189–90.

6. Hillel Geva, "Twenty-Five Years of Excavations in Jerusalem, 1967–1992," in Ancient Jerusalem Revealed, ed. Hillel Geva (Jerusalem: Israel Exploration Society, 2000), 18.

7. Kathleen M. Kenyon, *Digging up Jerusalem* (London: Ernest Benn Limited, 1974), 177.

8. Jane M. Cahill and David Tarler, "Excavations Directed by Yigal Shiloh at the City of David, 1978–1985," in *Ancient Jerusalem Revealed*, ed. Hillel Geva (Jerusalem: Israel Exploration Society, 2000), 39–40.

9. Eilat Mazar, *Discovering the Solomonic Wall in Jerusalem: A Remarkable Archaeological Adventure* (Jerusalem: Shoham Academic Research and Publication, 2011), 147–48.

10. Saïd Nuseibeh and Oleg Grabar, *The Dome of the Rock* (London: Thames and Hudson, 1996), 107-08.

11. Ibid.

An aerial view of Bethel, the House of God, where both Abraham and Jacob encountered God and built altars to worship and commemorate Him.

Chapter 3

THE GATE OF HEAVEN

Though the Bible was written in ancient times and spans thousands of years, we can still use its detailed descriptions to pinpoint where important events took place. Genesis 12:8 is a great example. In a single verse, we are given information about the location of three different sites.

> From there he [Abram] went on toward the hills east of Bethel and pitched his tent, with Bethel on the west and Ai on the east. There he built an altar to the LORD and called on the name of the LORD.

This verse mentions two cities, Bethel and Ai, and between them a campsite where Abram (Abraham) built an altar. Establishing where any one of these three sites was located enables us to identify the other two.

Img. 60: This photograph was shot in the 1890s and shows what the travel routes looked like before they became paved roads. Explorers Robinson and Smith traveled on horseback along these routes, just as ancient travelers would have.

BETHEL

In 1838 American scholar and explorer Edward Robinson, along with his traveling companion Eli Smith, rode horses into a town about twelve miles north of Jerusalem. The Arab residents called their town Beitin (*bayt een'*). Robinson and Smith were the first to make the linguistic connection that the Arabic name *Beitin* preserved the older Hebrew name *Bethel.* The names Bethel and Beitin both mean "House of God." Robinson and Smith's original claim that Beitin is Bethel, based on name preservation, was confirmed by later linguists. For example, Anson Rainey and Steven Notley state in their book, *The Sacred Bridge*, "The equation of Beitin with biblical Bethel is absolutely certain."[1]

Name preservation is not the only point we can use to accurately identify the city of Bethel. The Bible describes ancient travel routes passing through Bethel (see *Img. 60* and *Img. 61*), and those descriptions correspond with travel routes through Beitin that were still in use at the time of Robinson and Smith.

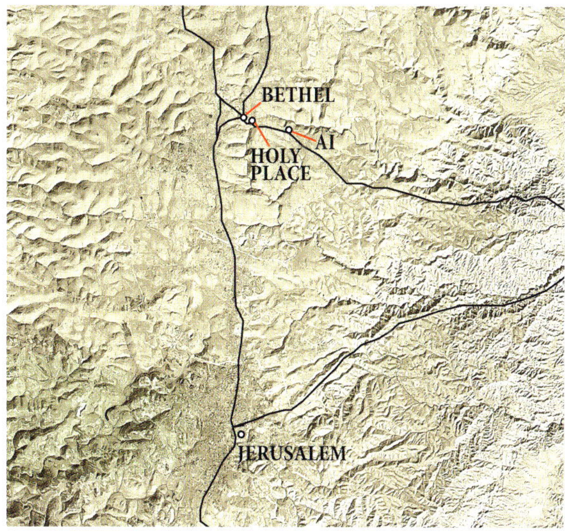

Img. 61: This map shows Bethel and Ai in proximity to Jerusalem.

Based on the strong linguistic and geographical evidence for identifying Beitin as Bethel, famous archaeologist William F. Albright began a preliminary dig at Beitin in 1927, with full-scale excavations starting in 1934. In his excavation report, Albright summed up the evidence his team uncovered at Beitin/Bethel as follows:

> The town was a flourishing Canaanite settlement, which was occupied more or less continually through the Patriarch and post-Patriarch (Middle and Late Bronze) Ages, at the close of which it was destroyed. It was an important town during Iron I (period of the Judges and United Mon-archy) and was almost continuously occupied through Iron II and down to the late sixth century. It was occupied in the Persian Period, in accordance with Ezra and Nehemiah. The vicissitudes of the site in the Hellenistic, Roman, and Byzantine Ages agree remarkably well with the literary sources . . . there can be no doubt, about the correctness of the identification of Beitin with Biblical Bethel.[2]

The archaeological layers found at Bethel match what would be expected at the site based on the history laid out in the Bible, particularly the Middle Bronze Age layer, concerning the time period of Abraham, Isaac, and Jacob.

Based on the combined evidence including name preservation, geography, and archaeology, scholars came to firm agreement that the small city of Beitin was the same location as the city of Bethel described in the Bible. Thus, Bethel was identified. And if Bethel's location is known, we can work from there to identify the location of Ai and then Abraham's campsite in between.

Img. 62: Excavations at Bethel began in 1934.

AI

Using Bethel as an anchor point, Genesis 12:8 makes the location of Ai obvious "with Bethel on the west and Ai on the east." Ai should be located fairly nearby and east of Bethel. There is only one ancient mound that fits this description: a ruin called Et-tell, which in Arabic means "the tel [ruin]." It is close to and directly east of Bethel, which is why Et-tell has long been identified by the majority of scholars as biblical Ai.

Like Bethel, this identification was confirmed through archaeology in 1928 when Et-tell was excavated by the well-known British archaeologist John Garstang. In his book *Joshua & Judges*, Garstang wrote about what he found there:

> Evidence was found of the occupation of the site in E.B.A. [Early Bronze Age]. While, as usual, M.B.A. [Middle Bronze Age] wares were most abundant, there was found a considerable proportion of L.B.A.i [Late Bronze Age I].[3]

Just as Albright had found evidence at Bethel, Garstang also found architectural and pottery evidence establishing that Ai was occupied during the time when Abraham, Isaac, and Jacob lived.

ABRAHAM'S ALTAR

With the two established anchor points of Bethel and Ai, let us read the Genesis account again, keeping in mind the place where Abraham built an altar.

> From there he [Abram] went on toward the hills east of Bethel and pitched his tent, with Bethel on the west and Ai on the east. There he built an altar to the LORD and called on the name of the LORD. (Genesis 12:8)

There is only one ruin between Bethel and Ai, located on top of a high ridge directly east of

Img. 63: Aerial view of Et-tell, which geography and archaeology have helped to identify as the city of Ai in Abraham's day. The road to Bethel is seen to the left of the ruins.

Bethel. This location matches the description in Genesis 12:8. The remains of a medieval tower mark the site, which locals call Burj Beitin, "Tower of Beitin."

Img. 64: The location of the holy place between Bethel and Ai.

After camping for a time in between Bethel and Ai, Abraham traveled south to the Negev and then into Egypt. He later returned to his Bethel campsite:

> From the Negev he went from place to place until he came to Bethel, to the place between Bethel and Ai where his tent had been earlier and where he had first built an altar. There Abram called on the name of the Lord. (Genesis 13:3-4)

It was here, after Abraham called on the name of the Lord, that God spoke to him again about the promise of offspring.

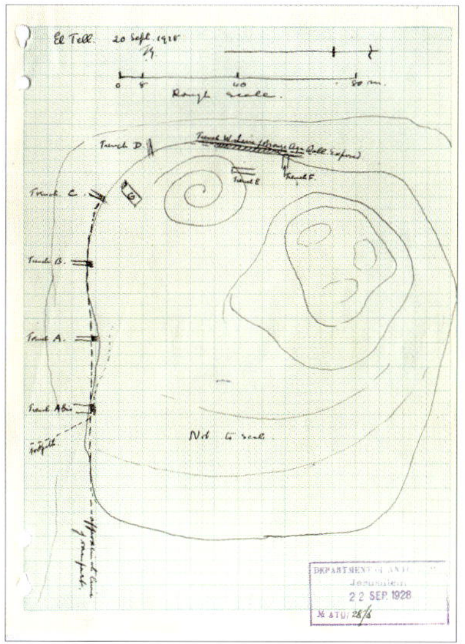

Img. 65: Garstang's drawing of Ai, showing where he excavated. (Courtesy of the IAA archives.)

Img. 66: Garstang marked and labeled a picture of Et-tell to identify the areas where he had excavated. (Courtesy of the IAA archives.)

> The Lord said to Abram, . . . "Look around from where you are, to the north and south, to the east and west. All the land that you see I will give to you and your offspring forever. I will make your offspring like the dust of the earth, so that if anyone could count the dust, then your offspring could be counted. Go, walk through the length and breadth of the land, for I am giving it to you." (Genesis 13:14-17)

Though Abraham still had no offspring, God promised that his offspring would be as numerous as the dust at this campsite east of Bethel. However, Abraham is not the only one God appeared to at this campsite. Abraham's grandson Jacob would also have an encounter with God on this same plot of ground.

JACOB'S ALTAR

In the archaeological layers beneath the ruin of the medieval tower at Burj Beitin, recent excavations have uncovered the foundations of a monumental Byzantine church dating to the fourth century AD.[4] The church ends in a single apse, seen in the wall-shaped half circle at the front of the building. This apse and the sheer size of the structure are hallmarks of a church built to commemorate a sacred event. But how can we know which sacred event this church commemorated?

The answer to this important question comes from Jerome, an early Christian leader (AD 347–420), who visited the church when it was relatively new and wrote the following: "There also is a church built where Jacob slept as he passed through to Mesopotamia, whence also he gave it the name Bethel, that is, House of God."[5]

Jerome's quote establishes that this is the site which was commemorated as the place Jacob named "the House of God." Let's look at Jacob's story:

> Jacob left Beersheba and set out for Haran. When he reached a certain place, he stopped for the night because the sun had set. Taking one of the stones there, he put it under his head and lay down to sleep. He had a dream in which he saw a stairway resting on the earth, with its top reaching to heaven, and the angels of God were ascending and descending on it. There above it stood the Lord, and he said: "I am the Lord, the God of your father Abraham and the God of Isaac. I will give you and your descendants the land on which you are lying. Your descendants will be like the dust of the earth, and you will spread out to the west and to the east, to the north and to the south. All peoples on earth will be blessed through you and your offspring." When Jacob awoke from his sleep, he thought, "Surely the Lord is in this place, and I was not aware of it." He was afraid and said, "How awesome is this place! This is none other than the house of God; this is the gate of heaven." Early the next morning Jacob took the stone he had placed under his head and set it up as a pillar and poured oil on top of it. He called that place Bethel, though the city used to be called Luz. (Genesis 28:10-14, 16-19)

Like Abraham, Jacob had a personal encounter with God at this campsite between Bethel (Luz) and Ai. The encounter shaped Jacob's future and established a sacred place for his coming descendants. The nearby city, which had been called Luz, would come to be identified with the site of Jacob's dream and also be called Bethel. That is why Bethel names both the nearby city and the spot where Jacob saw the entrance to "the House of God" and met the living God.

THE INTERPRETATION

On a hard plot of ground, with his head resting on a rock, Jacob dreamed of heaven opened. But his dream wouldn't be fully understood until thousands of years later when it would be explained to a Galilean fisherman named Nathanael. As he dreamed, Jacob saw a stairway reaching down from heaven to the plot of ground where he slept. Angels were coming and going on this

Img. 67: A straight-down aerial view of the recent excavations at the holy place east of Bethel and west of Ai. The square structure on the upper right side of the picture is the medieval tower. The town, Burj (tower) Beitin, is named in reference to that tower. Just to the left of the tower is the apse of the church, in the shape of a half circle, pointing east. The church's entrance is on the opposite, western side of the building. This monumental church building has commemorated and marked the authentic location of Abraham's campsite and Jacob's dream for over eighteen centuries.

BETHEL
CAMPSITE

Img. 68 (facing page, top): The location of the campsite (right foreground) fits perfectly with Genesis 12:8, which describes a place in "the hills east of Bethel . . . with Bethel on the west and Ai on the east" where Abraham camped, built an altar, and called upon the name of the Lord. Later, Abraham's grandson Jacob named the place Bethel, "the House of God," after the Lord appeared to him there in a dream. In the background (left of the site in the photo) is the present-day Palestinian town of Beitin. Note the minaret sticking up from the local mosque (left background). This mosque is near a spring of the ancient Canaanite city of Luz, which later came to be called Bethel by the Israelites because of its close proximity to Jacob's dream site.

Img. 69 (panorama at bottom): Bethel on the west (far left), Ai (Et-tell) on the east (far right), with Abraham and Jacob's campsite in between.

Img. 70 (directly below): Et-tell, the archaeological site of biblical Ai.

staircase, but Jacob did not approach to try to climb up himself. Instead, the Lord descended the staircase to meet with him and speak with him. God came down and spoke to Jacob.

In the very place where the LORD had spoken a promise to his grandfather Abraham, the LORD spoke the same promise to Jacob: his descendants would be as numerous as the dust and would inherit the land surrounding Bethel to the north, south, east, and west. Of all of these promised descendants, one would bring blessing to all people: "All peoples on earth will be blessed through you and your offspring" (Genesis 28:14).

When Jacob awoke, he "took the stone he had placed under his head and set it up as a pillar and poured oil on top of it" (Genesis 28:18), and before this anointed stone, Jacob made his own promise to the LORD:

> Then Jacob made a vow, saying, "If God will be with me and will watch over me on this journey I am taking and will give me food to eat and clothes to wear so that I return safely to my father's household, then the LORD will be my God." (Genesis 28:20-21)

Jacob left that spot and journeyed on to Haran where he worked, married, and had a family. After being in Haran for a long time, Jacob had another dream in which the LORD spoke with him. "I am the God of Bethel, where you made a vow to me. Now leave this land at once and go back to your native land" (Genesis 31:13).

After Jacob made his way back to the land of Canaan, the LORD spoke to him about Bethel again.

> Then God said to Jacob, "Go up to Bethel and settle there, and build an altar there to God, who appeared to you when you were fleeing from your brother Esau." Jacob and all the people with him came to Luz (that is, Bethel) in the land of Canaan. There he built an altar, and he called the place El Bethel [God of Bethel], because it was there that God revealed himself to him when he was fleeing from his brother.... God appeared to him again and blessed him. God said to him, "Your name is Jacob, but you will no longer be called Jacob; your name will be Israel." So he named him Israel. And God said to him, "I am God Almighty; be fruitful and increase in number. A nation and a community of nations will come from you, and kings will be among your descendants. The land I gave to Abraham and Isaac I also give to you, and I will give this land to your descendants after you." (Genesis 35:1, 6-7, 9-12)

After their first meeting, Jacob had made a vow that if God were faithful to him he would choose to serve Him as his God. In reality, God chose Jacob, calling him back to the land of his fathers, blessing him, and reaffirming his promise: Jacob's descendants would multiply to a community of nations, and the King-of-kings would come from him.

To signify the guaranteed success of His promise, God changed Jacob's name to Israel, which means "he who prevails with God." God's promise to Jacob would prevail. Jacob's very identity was changed because of this encounter. The LORD was no longer just the God of his fathers. Now the LORD was his God, the God of "Abraham, Isaac and Jacob" (Genesis 50:24).

The covenant promise had been given and received, and as he had done before,

> Jacob set up a stone pillar at the place God had talked with him, and he poured out a drink offering on it; he also poured oil on it. Jacob called where God had talked with him Bethel. (Genesis 35:14-15)

Jacob responded to God by erecting a standing stone to mark the place, a testimony to the promise given. The scene closes on a standing stone stained red with wine and dripping with oil, testifying of a promise made. Centuries passed. Jacob's descendants did become numerous, and in time the descendant who would bless "all peoples on earth" arrived—Jesus.

The beginning of the Gospel of John shows Jesus gathering disciples. He calls Philip to follow Him. Excited, Philip searches out his friend, Nathanael, to recruit him to follow as well. Finding Nathanael, Philip exclaims, "We have found the one Moses wrote about…Jesus of Nazareth" (John 1:45). Curious, Nathanael goes with Philip to see this person his friend is telling him about.

On meeting Nathanael, Jesus says to him, "Very truly I tell you, you will see 'heaven open, and the angels of God ascending and descending on the Son of Man'" (John 1:51). Jacob's descendant is quoting Jacob's dream. He's not just quoting it; he's placing himself in it! In essence, Jesus is telling Nathanael, "I am the stairway in Jacob's dream."

In the Person of Jesus, God had come down from heaven to earth. God had talked with Jacob and made him a promise in the same way Jesus talked with Nathanael, saying, "You will see heaven open." Just like Jacob, Nathanael knew he was in the presence of God. Nathanael declared, "Rabbi, you are the Son of God; you are the king of Israel" (John 1:49).

Jacob's promised King was now Nathanael's King! Just as Jacob chose to follow God, Nathanael chose to follow Jesus.

Jacob's dream and the holy place of Bethel are all about Jesus. Jesus was a living house of God: "The Word became flesh [who] made his dwelling among us" (John 1:14). Jesus was the gate into heaven of Jacob's dream: "I am the gate; whoever enters through me will be saved" (John 10:9). Jesus was the stairway connecting heaven and earth: "I am the way and the truth and the life. No one comes to the Father except through me" (John 14:6). In Jesus, God descended to earth, enabling man to ascend to heaven.

A standing stone still marks the spot where Jacob dreamed and God promised. The stones that stand there were not raised by Jacob, however. They are the stones of an ancient church which was built on the very spot where the LORD talked to Jacob and said, "All peoples on earth will be blessed through you and your offspring." Jacob's standing stone testified of God's promise to come. Today, those ancient church stones testify to the truth that God fulfilled His promise. Christ came. Men were washed in His blood, anointed with His Spirit, and blessed with eternal life.

NOTES

1. Anson F. Rainey and R. Steven Notley, *The Sacred Bridge: Carta's Atlas of the Biblical World* (Jerusalem: Carta, 2006), 116.

2. James L. Kelso, *The Excavation of Bethel (1934–1960)* (Cambridge: American Schools of Oriental Research, 1968), 3.

3. John Garstang, *The Foundations ofBible History: Joshua, Judges* (London: Constable & Co. Ltd., 1971), 356.

4. H. Kansha, "A Byzantine Church at Beitin, Palestine" (paper presented at the Archi-Cultural Interactions Through the Silk Road, 4th International Conference, Nishinomiya, Japan, July 16-18, 2016). At the time of this writing, the excavations at Burj Beitin directed by Kansha H. for Keio University were ongoing.

5. Eusebius et al., *The Onomasticon by Eusebius of Caesarea: Palestine in the Fourth Century A.D.* (Jerusalem: Carta, 2003), 13.

A shepherd leads his flock of sheep near the city of Hebron where Abraham, Isaac, and Jacob also tended their herds and flocks.

Chapter 4

THE SHEPHERD'S CAVE

Machpelah is the burial site of the biblical patriarchs and their wives. Although they were simply shepherds living in tents, not kings and queens living in palaces, their burial place is the second-most venerated holy place in Israel. Located near Mamre, Machpelah is just east of and next to the tel of the biblical city of Hebron. Because Abraham is a central figure in both Judaism and Islam, his burial site is divided in half, with one side functioning as a Jewish synagogue and the other as an Islamic mosque. The site was explored and published in the early 1900s, but ongoing tensions at Machpelah have prevented further excavations.[1] Regardless, Machpelah is an archaeological wonder.

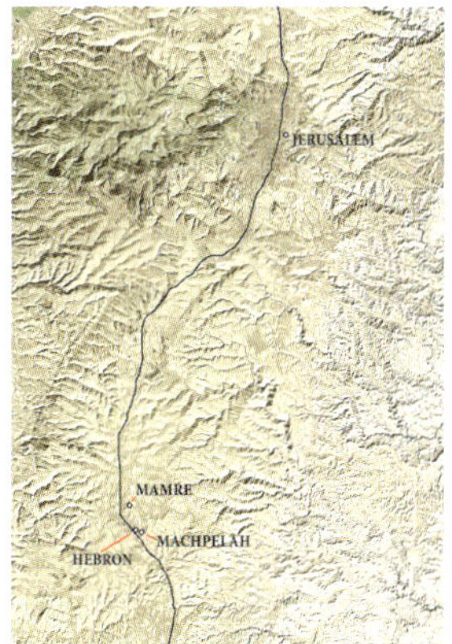

Img. 71: This is a map showing Machpelah just east of Hebron.

As we've discussed in the previous chapters, Herod the Great built up three holy places in Judea in order to please his Jewish subjects: Mamre, Moriah, and now the third—Machpelah. Herod enclosed all these sacred spaces with massive walls, using the same masonry style for each. From the time of their construction in the first century BC until now, the enclosure walls at Machpelah have remained the best preserved and are still standing mostly intact.

Herod built the walls around Mamre to enclose and commemorate Abraham's altar. In Jerusalem he expanded and enlarged the walls that enclosed the holy Mountain of Moriah. The enclosure walls built at Machpelah commemorate a cave. There are many caves in the rocky ridges surrounding Tel Hebron, but the story of Abraham tells us about just one of them. Do we know which particular cave the Bible is referring to? Yes, the cave surrounded by monumental walls that are more than two thousand years old.

To learn how this otherwise ordinary cave was transformed into a venerated holy place, we must again turn to the pages of Scripture. It begins with a matriarch of Israel:

Img. 72: Abraham, Isaac, and Jacob were buried in Machpelah cave, marked by the Herodian-walled structure seen in the center of photo.

Img. 73: This panoramic view shows the close proximity between the ancient city of Hebron and the cave of Machpelah.

Img. 74: An old photo of Hebron taken in 1945 with a close-up of Machpelah.

Img. 75: These are Herodian walls, best preserved at Machpelah.

Img. 76: Machpelah's masonry (pictured here), is identical to the masonry at the Western Wall in Jerusalem.

Img. 77: The red line delineates the height to which the Herodian walls are preserved. The masonry below the red line belongs to Herod the Great, while the masonry above the red line is later.

> Sarah lived to be a hundred and twenty-seven years old. She died at Kiriath Arba (that is, Hebron) in the land of Canaan, and Abraham went to mourn for Sarah and to weep over her. (Genesis 23:1-2)

Sarah, who had given birth to Isaac when she was over ninety years old, had perished.

> He [Abraham] said to them [inhabitants of Hebron], "If you are willing to let me bury my dead, then listen to me and intercede with Ephron son of Zohar on my behalf so he will sell me the cave of Machpelah."(Genesis 23:8-9)

A transaction takes place between Abraham and Ephron "in the hearing of all the Hittites who had come to the gate of his city [Hebron]" (Genesis 23:10).

> So Ephron's field in Machpelah near Mamre—both the field and the cave in it, and all the trees within the borders of the field—was deeded to Abraham as his property in the presence of all the Hittites who had come to the gate of the city. Afterward Abraham buried his wife Sarah in the cave in the field of Machpelah near Mamre (which is at Hebron) in the land of Canaan. So the field and the cave in it were deeded to Abraham by the Hittites as a burial site. (Genesis 23:17-20)

Even though the holy place of Machpelah has never been excavated, the ancient tel of Hebron has been. And while the city gate has not yet been located by archaeologists, sections of the city wall dating to the time of Abraham have been uncovered.[2]

The gate of this city wall is where Abraham transacted his purchase, the only land Abraham ever owned in Canaan. This one small burial plot pointed toward the LORD's promise: in the future Abraham's offspring would possess all of the land of Canaan.

Herod's towering enclosure walls mark this field and cave as the authentic location of the patriarchal burial site. It is no wonder that Jews today consider it the second holiest place in the world.

As was customary, Sarah's body would have been laid out within the tomb and left there. Over the course of about a year, her body would have decomposed, leaving only her bones. After the time of interment was over, her bones would have been gathered and situated in the cave. And, as was also the custom in ancient times, Abraham had purchased this cave not just for Sarah's burial alone but also for himself. This would be a family burial site to be used for generations to come.

> Abraham left everything he owned to Isaac. Abraham lived a hundred and seventy-five years. Then Abraham breathed his last and died at a good old age, an old man and full of years; and he was gathered to his people. His sons Isaac and Ishmael buried him in the cave of Machpelah near Mamre, in the field of Ephron son of Zohar the Hittite, the

Img. 78: Just as Herod built monumental walls around Abraham's altar at Mamre, he also built the same style of commemorative walls around Abraham's burial site at Machpelah.

Img. 79: A section of the ancient city wall of Hebron.

> field Abraham had bought from the Hittites. There Abraham was buried with his wife Sarah. After Abraham's death, God blessed his son Isaac. (Genesis 25:5, 7-11)

Two of Abraham's offspring, Isaac and Ishmael, buried him with his wife Sarah, but only one of these sons of Abraham was also Sarah's son. Miraculously born to a barren woman who was long past the age of childbearing, Isaac was the promised son.

Img. 80: An Old Testament Period tomb excavated in Jerusalem. Notice the burial bench where bodies of recently deceased family members would have been placed as their bodies decayed to bones.

Img. 81: Directly below the burial bench is a carved-out area called a repository. Once the deceased's body had turned to only bones, their bones were thrown in with those of their ancestors—as Genesis puts it, "gathered to their people." This was the burial custom practiced by Abraham and his family in the cave of Machpelah.

This is the reason that only Isaac was buried with his parents in the cave of Machpelah.

> Jacob came home to his father Isaac in Mamre, near Kiriath Arba (that is, Hebron), where Abraham and Isaac had stayed. Isaac lived a hundred and eighty years. Then he breathed his last and died and was gathered to his people, old and full of years. And his sons Esau and Jacob buried him. (Genesis 35:27-29)

Isaac was buried by his two sons, Jacob and Esau, and Scripture says Isaac "was gathered to his people." Archaeology can help us understand what this means. Through excavations of Old Testament Period family tombs, we see how generations of descendants were buried.

Each deceased family member was laid in a tomb and left to decay. After a period of about a year, their bones were gathered and placed into a pile of bones, together with family members who had died before them. Their bones were literally gathered to the bones of their ancestors. The bones of Isaac were gathered into the pile of his parents and laid among the bones of Abraham and Sarah.

Sometime after burying his father, Jacob moved his family to Egypt to escape a severe famine. In Egypt, the aging Jacob knew his time was drawing to an end. But God had promised Abraham that "all peoples on earth will be blessed through you and your offspring" (Genesis 28:14), and Jacob knew that this promise would not die with him. Jacob knew he too would soon be gathered to his forefathers, but which of his twelve sons would inherit the immortal promise?

Just before he died, Jacob blessed each of his sons. The blessing which he gave Judah, his fourth son and one of the sons of Leah, revealed that the promised offspring would come through his descendants.

> "The scepter will not depart from Judah, nor the ruler's staff from between his feet, until he to whom it belongs shall come and the obedience of the nations shall be his." (Genesis 49:10)

THE SCEPTER

Img. 82: An Assyrian king holding his scepter.

Img. 83: A gold scepter, discovered in the tomb of an Egyptian king.

Img. 84: Many stone reliefs discovered in the palaces of Assyrian kings contain human figures. How do we know which of these figures is the king? The king is the one holding the scepter. When Jacob spoke of a scepter in his blessing to Judah, he was declaring that a king would come from Judah's lineage.

Img. 85: A king displays his royal power by wielding his scepter.

THE ROYAL STAFF

Img. 89: A Persian king with his staff between his feet.

Imgs. 86, 87, 88: (Above, left to right) A shepherd, an Egyptian king, and an Assyrian king, all holding their staff at their feet. The shepherd uses his staff to direct and lead his sheep. The kings above hold both a scepter and a royal staff because they are also to protect as they lead and direct their people. The ancient concept of a shepherd-king is what is pictured in Jacob's blessing over his son Judah. Judah was a shepherd at the time he received the prophetic, royal blessing

Who is this king that would come from the line of Judah? Genesis 49:10 says, "The scepter would not depart from Judah, nor the ruler's staff from between his feet." The blessing states that not only would the kingly line come from Judah, the kingly authority would never depart "until he to whom it belongs shall come and the obedience of the nations shall be his." The ruler that would come from Judah would be eternal and king over the whole world.

This blessing became a tremendous source of hope for Israel, anchoring their expectation that this coming king would be their Messiah.

Img. 90: Present-day Machpelah.

After Jacob finished blessing his sons, he made his final request:

> Then he gave them these instructions: "I am about to be gathered to my people. Bury me with my fathers in the cave in the field of Ephron the Hittite, the cave in the field of Machpelah, near Mamre in Canaan, which Abraham bought along with the field as a burial place from Ephron the Hittite. There Abraham and his wife Sarah were buried, there Isaac and his wife Rebekah were buried, and there I buried Leah." (Genesis 49:29-31)

Here Jacob recounts the lineage of bones to which he will soon be gathered. Neither Ishmael nor Esau were buried there. Nor was Jacob's beloved wife Rachel. However, Leah, Judah's mother, was buried at Machpelah, and soon the bones of her husband would join hers.

> When Jacob had finished giving instructions to his sons, he drew his feet up into the bed, breathed his last and was gathered to his people. So Jacob's sons did as he had commanded them: They carried him to the land of Canaan and buried him in the cave in the field of Machpelah, near Mamre. (Genesis 49:33, 50:12-13)

Centuries later, the field and cave of Machpelah would become the inheritance of Judah's descendants, and ultimately Judah would become a kingdom, with its capital located in Hebron. The great and famous King David would begin his rule from there and build his palace overlooking the burial cave of his ancestors. From this vantage point, King David could ponder what his ancestor Jacob had promised: that in the fullness of time, another king would come from that lineage of bones, but this King would rule over all the world.

NOTES

1. For early archaeological explorations and descriptions of Machpelah see L. H. Vincent, E. J. H. Mackay, and F. M. Abel, *Hébron: Le Haram El-Khalîl: Sépulture Des Patriarches* (Paris: Ernest Leroux, 1923).

2. For the archaeology of Hebron see Philip C. Hammond, "An American Expedition to Hebron" (project prospectus, Brandeis University, 1964), 48–63. See also Jeffrey R. Chadwick, "The Archaeology of Biblical Hebron in the Bronze and Iron Ages: An Examination of the Discoveries of the American Expedition to Hebron" (PhD diss., University of Utah, 1992).

An aerial view of the City of David, from the Siloam Pool (unexcavated) at the bottom point, looking up the hill to the Temple Mount.

Chapter 5

THE COVENANT CITY

In 2005, Hebrew University professor Eilat Mazar excavated the acropolis of the City of David, uncovering massive walls of a monumental building. Mazar interpreted these walls to belong to an administrative building which had stood atop the city. While the pottery found within these foundational structures provided approximate dates for the building's construction, the questions remained: Who built the building? Who lived in it? What happened there?

To answer these questions, Mazar turned to the Bible:

> Now Hiram, King of Tyre, sent envoys to David, along with cedar logs and carpenters and stonemasons, and they built a palace for David. Then David knew that the LORD had established him as king over Israel and had exalted his kingdom for the sake of his people Israel. (2 Samuel 5:11-12)

Using these verses, Mazar interpreted this important find in her excavation report:

> [O]n the basis of the finds . . . we were left with a range indicating a date circa 1000 BCE . . . The historical description in II Samuel 5 of David and his Phoenician allies—those reputable builders who constructed his new palace—is immeasurably well suited to the archaeological facts uncovered in the excavations of the Large Stone Structure . . . the Large Stone Structure should be identified with King David's palace.[1]

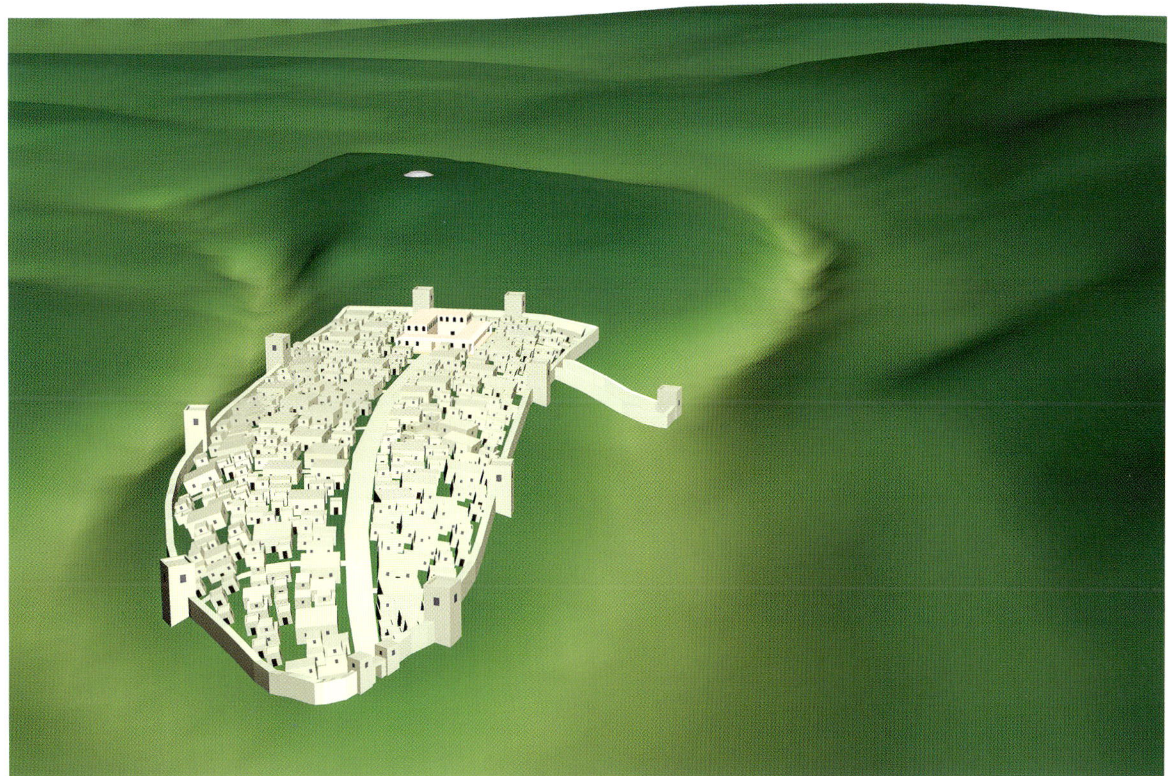

Img. 91: A model depicting the topography surrounding the City of David in ancient times. Compare it to the present-day City of David on the facing page.

DAVID'S PALACE

Mazar's words provide an excellent example of how biblical archaeology should work. Where mute, stone structures cannot explain their purpose or context, the Bible can.

Scripture informs us that long ago, within these very walls, an eternal covenant was forged:

> After the king [David] was settled in his palace and the LORD had given him rest from all his enemies around him, he said to Nathan the prophet, "Here I am, living in a house of cedar, while the ark of God remains in a tent." Nathan replied to the king, "Whatever you have in mind, go ahead and do it, for the LORD is with you." But that night the word of the LORD came to Nathan, saying: "Go and tell my servant David, 'This is what the LORD says: Are you the one to build me a house to dwell in?...the LORD declares to you that the LORD himself will establish a house for you: When your days are over and you rest with your ancestors, I will raise up

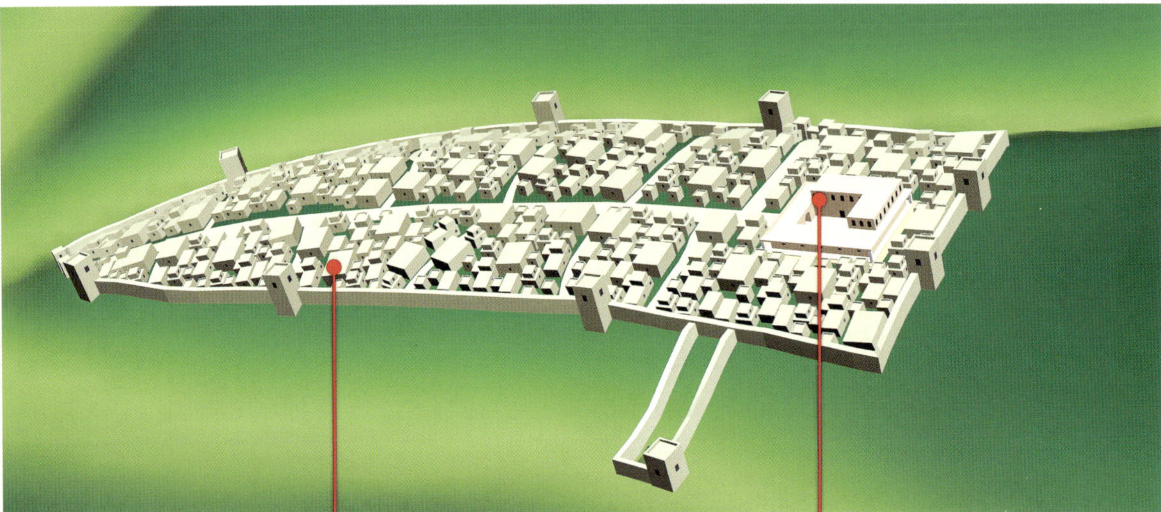

Img. 92: This illustration shows the location of David's palace at the upper end of he City of David.

Img. 93: An aerial photo of the location where the foundations of David's palace were discovered in excavations.

your offspring to succeed you, your own flesh and blood, and I will establish his kingdom. He is the one who will build a house for my Name, and I will establish the throne of his kingdom forever. I will be his father, and he will be my son. When he does wrong, I will punish him with a rod wielded by men, with floggings inflicted by human hands. But my love will never be taken away from him, as I took it away from Saul, whom I removed from before you. Your house and your kingdom will endure forever before me; your throne will be established forever.'" (2 Samuel 7:1-5, 11-16)

Img. 94: A closer look at one of the walls that contained pottery, dating its construction to the time of David in the tenth century BC.

Here the Hebrew word *beit*, translated as "house," has a dual meaning. David's covenant included promises about two different houses. One house was a "dwelling place," the other a "dynasty." The house David desired to build for the LORD's dwelling place was a building, a temple to hold the presence of God. The house the LORD desired to build for David was a royal dynasty, a lineage of sons to sit on David's throne. So which house is more important, the house of the LORD or the house of David? Certainly the house of the LORD sounds greater. However, the true significance is not in who the house is built for, but rather in who the builder is. What man builds is temporal. What God builds is eternal, for "everything God does will endure forever" (Ecclesiastes 3:14).

Solomon would build a temple for the LORD, and the LORD would establish a dynasty for David. In response to this, David humbly prayed.

> "And now, LORD God, keep forever the promise you have made concerning your servant and his house . . . LORD Almighty, God of Israel, you have revealed this to your servant, saying, 'I will build a house for you.'" (2 Samuel 7:25, 27)

Img. 95: The foundation walls of the monumental building that Dr. Mazar unearthed and identified as David's palace.

TOMB OF DAVID

While God's promise to David was that his offspring would rule forever, the LORD clearly told David that this promise to him would be fulfilled after his lifetime: "When your days are over and you rest with your ancestors" (2 Samuel 7:12).

In 1913 the first Jewish archaeologist to excavate in Jerusalem, Raymond Weill, began a quest to find the royal tombs of the house of David. Two verses informed him where to dig. The first was from 1 Kings 2:10: "Then David rested with his ancestors and was buried in the City of David."

The Law of Moses deemed dead bodies as unclean, causing those who came into contact with them to be defiled; so the dead were buried outside Israelite cities. The burial of kings, however, was the exception. First Kings 2:10 informed Weill that David's tomb was located somewhere within the roughly eleven-acre area of the City of David. If he could find tombs dating to the Israelite Period, then by Mosaic Law, they would be the tombs of kings. And since David's dynasty ruled from Jerusalem, such tombs would have to be those of the house of David.

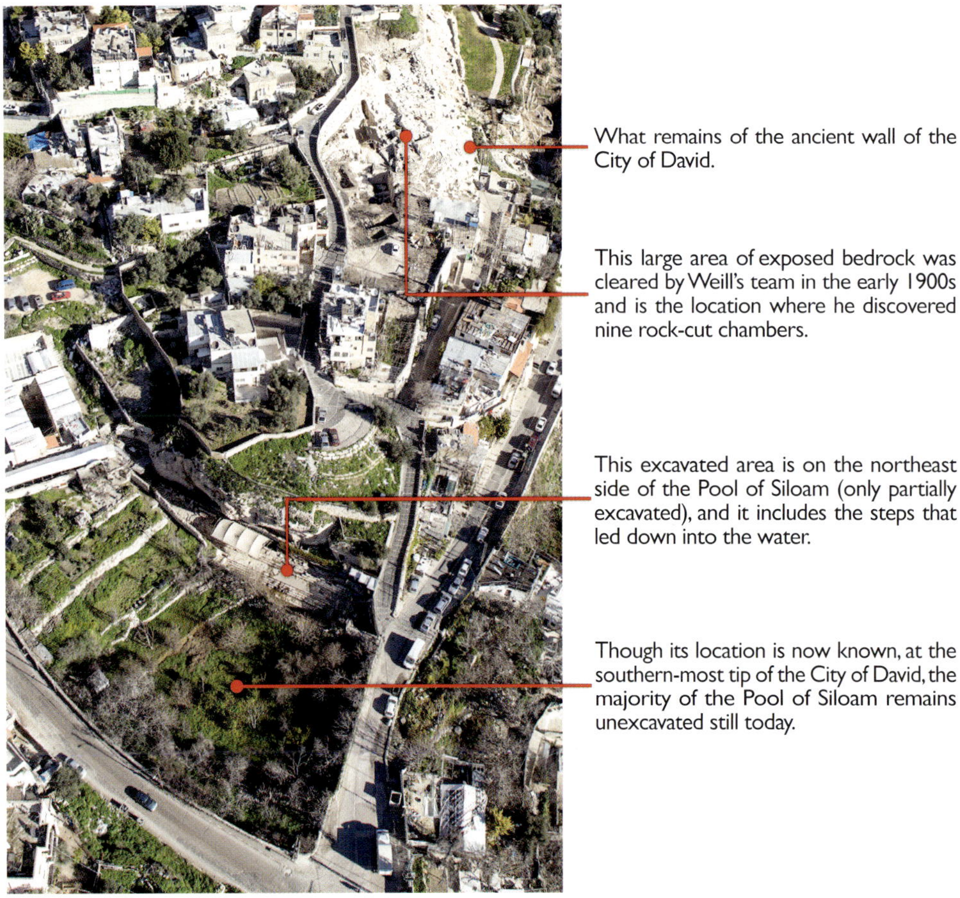

The book of Nehemiah supplied Weill with the second piece of information he needed to narrow down his excavation area. In the Persian Period, Nehemiah returned to Jerusalem to rebuild the city walls, which were still mainly in ruins from the Babylonian destruction. Each section of wall reconstruction was overseen by the head of a family and the work carried out by the members of his family.

> Shallun . . . repaired the wall of the Pool of Siloam, by the King's Garden, as far as the steps going down from the City of David. Beyond him, Nehemiah son of Azbuk . . . made repairs up to a point opposite the tombs of David, as far as the artificial pool. (Nehemiah 3:15-16)

What remains of the ancient wall of the City of David.

This large area of exposed bedrock was cleared by Weill's team in the early 1900s and is the location where he discovered nine rock-cut chambers.

This excavated area is on the northeast side of the Pool of Siloam (only partially excavated), and it includes the steps that led down into the water.

Though its location is now known, at the southern-most tip of the City of David, the majority of the Pool of Siloam remains unexcavated still today.

Img. 96: An aerial view of the present day City of David.

The context of Nehemiah 3 makes it clear that these verses are part of a description of the rebuilding of the city wall, beginning at the southern tip of the City of David and moving north along the eastern city wall. The section of wall being rebuilt in verse 15 begins at the pool of Siloam and ends at steps. While these steps have not been found through archaeology, the Pool of Siloam has been.

Img. 97: Aerial view looking down on the area that Weill's team cleared, showing the two most intact tombs they unearthed.

The next section described in verse 16 begins at these unknown steps and continues further north towards the Temple Mount up to "a point opposite the tombs of David, as far as the artificial pool." Based on this information, Weill estimated where the royal tombs should be located. He then began to excavate a much larger area so as to be sure to include the place described in Nehemiah 3:16.

Employing two hundred local workers and thirty donkeys, Weill's team cleared the entire area down to bedrock.[2] Here, precisely where he expected, Weill discovered the remains of nine tombs in front of an ancient pool. The tombs themselves were greatly damaged because Romans had quarried the area for stone to build Aelia Capitolina. For some of the nine, only an indention marking the footprint of the original tomb remained. However, considerable portions of the two most monumental tombs were clearly visible.

In his excavation report, Weill described what his team unearthed:

> We discovered and have completely cleared what remains of a group of large tombs cut in horizontal galleries. . . . The location of the group, in the old city and adjoining the enclosure wall, corresponds perfectly to the few particulars that we have, mainly from Nehemiah, about

Img. 98: The royal tomb area from ground level, looking north toward the Temple Mount in the background.

> the situation of the Davidic necropolis. ...These funeral deposits are certainly from the Judean royal period.[3]

The most monumental and intact of the nine tombs Weill discovered was the one he labeled T1 (*Tomb 1*). Located at the end of its horizontal shaft is a carved-out depression as described by Weill in his report:

> Just at the end of T1, the high tunnel of the first stage retains its sarcophagus, hollowed out in the form of a trough... and one should see it as the resting place of the owner of the tomb.... Perhaps David was laid to rest in the excavated sarcophagus of the old upper tunnel of the T1 tomb.[4]

This carved trough at the back of T1 where the deceased would have been laid matched the sizes of other such troughs found in nearby tombs across the Kidron Valley.[5] Unlike modern burial custom where bodies are laid out full-length on their backs, in these early periods bodies were most often buried in a curled-up position on their side. The size of the carved-out burial niche in Tomb 1 would have accommodated this type of burial practice.

Img. 99: Looking through the entrance of Tomb 1 (foreground), the most monumental of the nine tombs Weill discovered in the City of David. Originally a complete subterranean shaft, now the middle portion is exposed to the sky, having been destroyed by stone cutters in the time of Hadrian.

In addition to being located inside the City of David, the tombs Weill discovered were unusual in another way. Customarily during this time period, tombs were communal, family tombs where multiple generations of family were buried together. The tombs Weill uncovered were not like the many family tombs commonly found outside of the city. Each one of these tombs had been constructed for a single person, which strengthened Weill's understanding that these tombs were for royal personages. This finding precisely matches the prophet Isaiah's description of the royal tombs in his scroll, "All the kings of the nations lie in state, each in his own tomb" (Isaiah 14:18).

So, according to this verse, we should expect the tomb of David to contain only his bones, in contrast to the multiple burials in the family tomb of Machpelah.

Weill's conclusion that he had found the tombs of the house of David was widely accepted by

Img. 100: This photo shows the back portion of Tomb 1 where the ceiling is preserved.

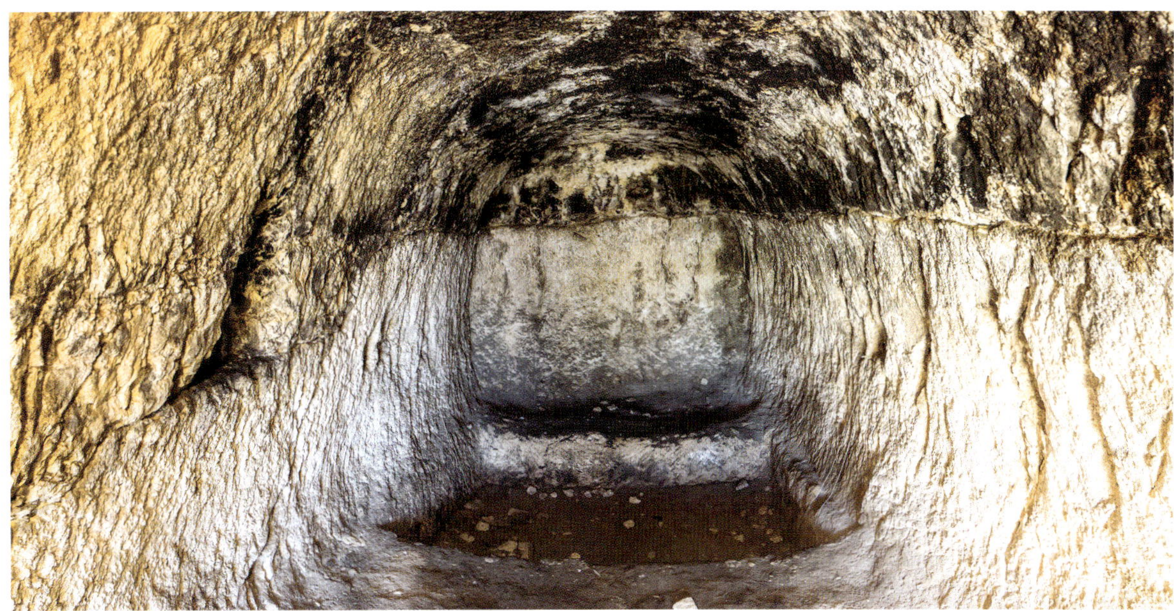

Img. 101: The burial niche at the very back of Tomb 1.

Img. 102: A close-up of the carved trough at the back of the horizontal shaft, the most likely place where the bones of King David were laid.

Img. 103: This photo shows how people were often buried in Old Testament times: in a curled position. The carved trough at the back of Tomb 1 is easily large enough to hold a corpse buried in this way.

his colleagues. However, this scholarly majority view began to change after the War of Independence in 1948 brought political upheaval. Israel was again a nation; however, Jerusalem was divided, and the City of David was part of the country of Jordan. Tensions ran high and affected archaeology in Israel.

In the 1960s, archaeologist Kathleen Kenyon excavated the City of David through the Jordan Antiquities Authority. Unfortunately, her archaeological interpretations led to the overturning of Weill's earlier assertions about the royal tombs being those of the Davidic family. It seems likely that Kenyon's conclusions were based more on the political situation at the time than on evidence. Below is a direct quote of Kenyon's from her book *Digging Up Jerusalem*:

> The controversial point is the cuttings that Weill identified as the Royal Tombs of the House of David. The Biblical evidence that David and his heirs were buried *in* Jerusalem has stimulated many searches and fanciful identifications, including that of the so-called Tomb of David shown to tourists today. The particular cuttings revealed by Weill were certainly unusual, consisting of two rock-cut tunnels side by side. They are not like any observed cisterns, though the plaster that covers the rock shows that they were at some stage used as cisterns.[6]

Kenyon's rebuttal of Weill was that these "rock-cut tunnels" should be understood to be cisterns. To suggest that these horizontal, cut-out tunnels were used as cisterns to hold water is highly improbable. There have been no other archaeological finds of horizontally-constructed water cisterns. All cisterns are dug vertically so that they can hold water.

In academic work, scholarship often bends to the pressures of politics and power. At the time of Kenyon's work, the political situation did not afford an interpretation of the tombs that accommodated a biblical understanding. Thus, Kenyon's baseless claim overtook Weill's scripturally-based interpretation. Despite this, the

Img. 104: Kenyon's interpretation, that the horizontal shaft (above) of Weill's Tomb 1 is a cistern, lacks credibility. His original identification remains the strongest—that this long shaft, ending with a carved-out trough, is a tomb. The evidence supports Weill: the tomb's location is precisely where the Bible says it should be, and parallel troughs, like the one found at the back of Tomb 1, were also found in other nearby tombs.

logical resting place for the bones of David is within the carved-out trough at the back of the most monumental tomb that Weill unearthed in the City of David.

THE INTERPRETATION

The significance behind the discovery of David's palace and his tomb is summed up in Psalm 16:

> Therefore my heart is glad and my tongue rejoices; my body also will rest secure, because you will not abandon me to the realm of the dead, nor will you let your faithful one see decay. You make known to me the path of life. (Psalm 16:9-11)

Is David writing about himself or someone else? He could not have been referring to himself because David perished and his body did decay in the grave. His flesh turned to bones and his bones to dust. This is what the LORD told David would happen according to the promise God made to David in his Jerusalem palace:

> "The Lord declares to you that the Lord himself will establish a house for you: When your days are over and you rest with your ancestors [emphasis added], I will raise up your offspring to succeed you, your own flesh and blood, and I will establish his kingdom." (2 Samuel 7:11-12)

After David was in the grave, his offspring would come and fulfill the promise. If the promise was to have been fulfilled by David or his son Solomon, all hope would have died and been buried with them.

For centuries after David's death, however, the Israelites continued to remember the promise given to David as they looked for the Son of David who was to come. Psalm 89 explains Israel's future hope:

> You said, "I have made a covenant with my chosen one, I have sworn to David my servant, 'I will establish your line forever and make your throne firm through all generations.' . . . And I will appoint him to be my firstborn, the most exalted of the kings of the earth. I will maintain my love to him forever, and my covenant with him will never fail. I will establish his line forever, his throne as long as the heavens endure. . . . Once for all, I have sworn by my holiness—and I will not lie to David—that his line will continue forever and his throne endure before me like the sun; it will be established forever like the moon, the faithful witness in the sky." (Psalm 89:3-4, 27-29, 35-37)

Who would be this "most exalted of the kings of the earth"? The one whose covenant with God "will never fail." The hope in this Psalm was not the dead king David but his coming offspring whom God would "raise up."

This offspring would not be abandoned to the grave. The one descending from David's lineage would not suffer decay. This coming, eternal King was the one which the Israelites would be expecting—their Messiah, the Son of David.

NOTES

1. Eilat Mazar, *The Palace of King David: Exca- vations at the Summit of the City of David; Preliminary Report of the Seasons 2005–2007* (Jerusalem: Shoham Academic Research and Publication, 2009), 53, 54, 64. See also Eilat Mazar et al., *The Summit of the City of David, Excavations 2005–2008: Final Reports Volume I* (Jerusalem: Shoham Academic Research and Publication, 2015).

2. Raymond Weill and L. H. Vincent, *The City of David: Revisiting Early Excavations; English Translations of Reports by Raymond Weill and L. H. Vincent*, ed. Hershel Shanks (Washington, D.C.: Biblical Archaeology Society, 2004), 15, 20.

3. Ibid., 21–23.

4. Ibid., 68, 76.

5. Hershel Shanks, "The Tombs of Silwan," *Biblical Archaeology Review* 20, no. 3, May/June (1994): 51.

6. Kenyon, *Digging Up Jerusalem*, 31–32.

PART II
NEW TESTAMENT
HOLY PLACES

From Tel Megiddo (pictured here), the modern city of Nazareth lies in the distance on the far side of the Jezreel Valley. By the Roman Period in the first century AD, the Old Testament city of Megiddo had long been in ruins.

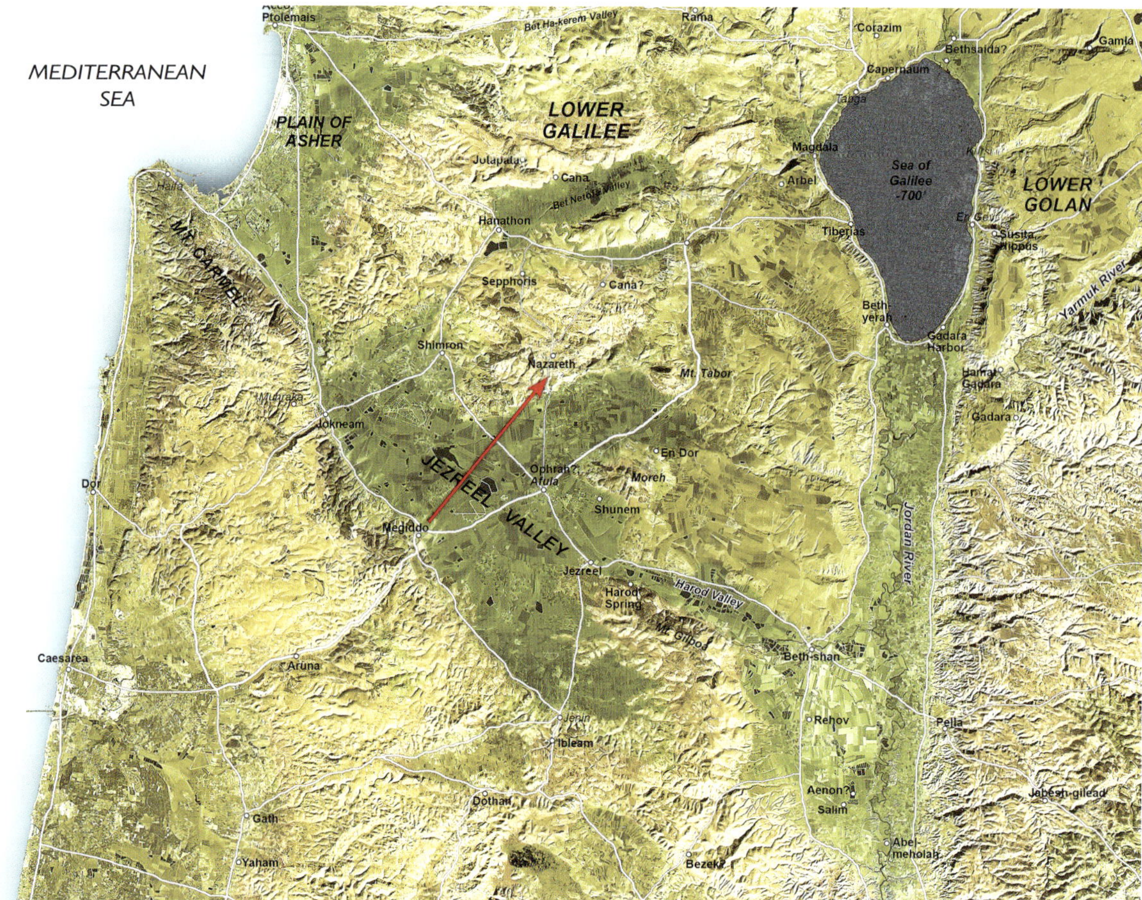

Img. 105: This map shows the location of Nazareth in the region of Galilee. The red arrow identifies the orientation of the picture on the previous page: looking to the north, across Tel Megiddo, toward Nazareth on the far side of the Jezreel Valley.

Img. 106: Taken in the early 1900s, this picture shows the road leading to and from Nazareth, which can be seen in the background spread out on the hill.

Chapter 6

THE HOUSE OF THE VIRGIN

Nazareth, one of the largest Palestinian cities in Israel today, is located in the hills to the north of the Jezreel Valley. At the base of the ridgeline cutting through the modern city is a spring, which has flowed for thousands of years. Situated nearby and just to the south of this water source is the largest church in the Middle East. The church's significance is not its size but rather the holy ground upon which it stands. What is this holy ground? To find the answer, we must peel back the archaeological layers one at a time.

THE MODERN CHURCH OF THE ANNUNCIATION (AD 1960 to Present)

The construction of the Church of the Annunciation, the massive building currently standing in the heart of Nazareth, was finished in 1960. This church continues to be a landmark and the main attraction for the city's visitors.

THE OLDER CHURCH OF THE ANNUNCIATION (AD 1730–AD 1954)

Preceding the modern church was an older church built in AD 1730. The earliest excavations in Nazareth were forced to dig around this building. However, the church was demolished in 1954 to prepare for the building of the new and larger church. Beginning in 1955, once the debris had been removed from the site, archaeologist Bellarimo Begatti began excavating. Now archaeologists could excavate newly exposed areas without a church building in the way.

Img. 107: This picture, taken in 1898, shows the older Church of the Annunciation, which was built in 1730.

Img. 108: The current Church of the Annunciation (pointed grey dome in center-right foreground) is seen with the modern city of Nazareth surrounding it and the Jezreel Valley in the background to the south.

CRUSADER CHURCH (c. AD 1105–AD 1263)

Img. 109: Rendering of Crusader church layer.

Below the level of the AD 1730 church were the ruins of a Crusader church (plan in green). It was built in the early part of the twelfth century AD, at some point before AD 1106 when it is first mentioned in a historical source.[1] Enough of the foundations of walls belonging to this church were preserved for the archaeologists to draw up a plan of the building. In typical Crusader style, this church building ends in three apses with rounded walls pointing toward the east. This church was violently destroyed by Sultan Baibars in AD 1263 and lay in ruins until AD 1730, when the new church was built over its ruins.[2]

BYZANTINE CHURCH (Early Fifth Century AD–AD 1009)

Img. 110: Rendering of Byzantine-Period layer.

Buried underneath the Crusader-Period ruins, archaeologists unearthed parts of an earlier church built during the Byzantine Period (plan in red), in the early part of the fifth century AD. A portion of the north apse was found preserved, along with enough parts of the foundational walls to allow for a reconstruction of the church's structural plan. Like the Crusader church before it, this earlier apse of the Byzantine church faced east toward the rising sun. A portion of the mosaic floor of the Byzantine church was also found in its original place.[3] The orientation of this Byzantine floor and its decoration are toward the east like the building it belongs to.

SYNAGOGUE/CHURCH (Second Century AD–Early Fifth Century AD)

Img. 111: Rendering of Jewish synagogue layer.

The evidence for a Jewish synagogue (plan in gray) was discovered in the layers below the remaining structures of the Byzantine church. As should be expected, with each descending layer, the architecture from previous buildings is unfortunately less well-preserved, damaged by the structures built on top of it. The result of this damage is that not enough architectural remains were found from the early Byzantine building to allow for a complete drawing of its basic structure.

However, there is no doubt that a building stood here beginning in the second century AD. We know this building existed by the parts of it that were found during excavations: columns, column bases, capitals, cornices, decorated stones, and one remaining wall. Just as pottery shards point to the existence of the pot they came from, the architectural remains that were uncovered speak to the reality that a second-century synagogue building once stood on this spot. In addition, this building's masonry style matches that of synagogues constructed in the Galilee region at that time.[4]

Img. 112: This is an example of an inscription on plaster found in excavations at Nazareth.

Img. 113: The Mosaic floor uncovered by Bagatti's excavation.

Amazingly, all of this evidence came together to reveal that underneath the remains of three layers of Christian churches was a Jewish synagogue. This spot had been venerated through many centuries, first by Jews and then by Christians. Fortunately, discoveries made during the excavations provided helpful information to explain what these Jews believed and why they built a synagogue over this particular place. Inscriptions were discovered on plaster belonging to this early synagogue building. One identified the name "Jesus" and another was translated as "rejoice Mary." Cross symbols, which would only be used by those who believed Jesus of Nazareth to be the Messiah, were also found.[5]

Img. 114 (above) and Img. 115 (below): The two monograms in the mosaics use the Greek letter Chi (Χ), the first letter in the Greek spelling of Christ (Χϱιστός), to form a cross. The vertical shaft of the cross also forms a Greek Rho (ϱ), which is the second letter in Christ (Χϱιστός). These monograms clearly represent the name Jesus Christ. Amazingly, they were discovered on the mosaic floor of a Jewish synagogue, beneath a later mosaic church floor. This evidence shows that the Jews who built and worshiped in this synagogue were Jewish followers of Christ.

Portions of another mosaic floor were found below the Byzantine floor, and surprisingly it proved to be the floor of a synagogue. Also unexpectedly, this floor was oriented toward the south, in contrast to the Byzantine mosaic floor above it, which was oriented toward the east. The church was oriented toward the rising sun, but why did the synagogue point south? Because the holy city of Jerusalem is located south of Nazareth and many synagogues were oriented toward Jerusalem.

Mosaic decorations were incorporated into portions of this south-oriented synagogue floor, including various crosses. One became known as the Mosaic of the Crown, shaped by using letters from the name Christ and encircled by a crown, reflecting a belief that Jesus Christ is King.

Img. 116: A weakness of archaeology is that it is destructive by nature. Higher layers have to be dismantled and removed in order to explore the archaeological layers below them. During this process, the evidence that is found and removed is recorded in excavation reports. Sometimes excavators find a way to leave some portions of earlier layers intact. Care was taken in the construction of The Church of the Annunciation to protect these intact areas so that visitors can still see the Jewish mikvah (a ritual bath area) which was uncovered, as well as several preserved patches of mosaic from the synagogue floor.

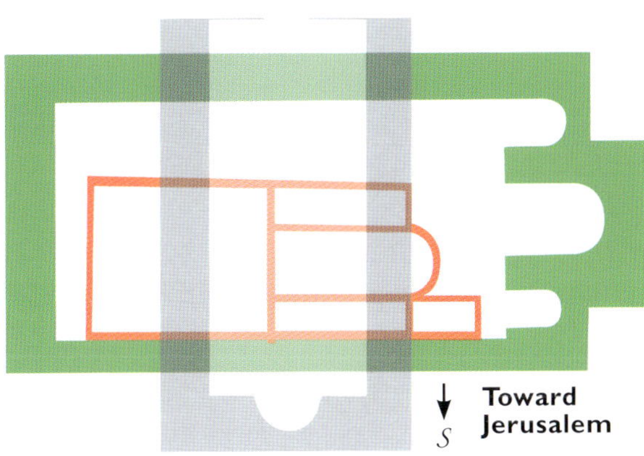

Img. 117: Each structure's building plan, showing their directional orientation, stacked on top of each other, with the synagogue (grey) being the bottom-most structure.

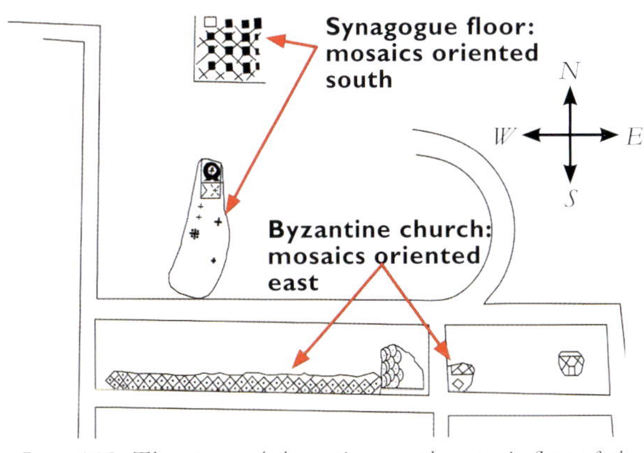

Img. 118: The apse and decorations on the mosaic floor of the church are oriented toward the east. In contrast, the decorations of the mosaics from the lower floor of the synagogue are oriented toward Jerusalem to the south.

Img. 119: Panoramic view of the inside of the modern Church of the Annunciation, identifying the locations of preserved archaeological features.

Based on this abundant evidence, Bagatti stressed that the initial builders of the synagogue were a people of "purely Jewish" culture who worshiped Jesus as their Messiah.[6] Bagatti therefore refers to them in his reports as Judeo-Christians and the building they built as a synagogue church in order to better communicate both their Jewishness and their Christian beliefs.[7]

Img. 120: A close-up view of the Jewish mikvah discovered at the lowest level of Bagatti's excavation at Nazareth.

Img. 121: Pottery vessels and lamps from the first century AD, found in excavations at Nazareth and on display in the archaeological museum located next to the Church of the Annunciation.

FIRST CENTURY AD HOUSE

So far we've looked at the layers under the modern church to see three Christian churches and a synagogue-church. But what lies at the very bottom of this stack of archaeological layers? A house dating to the first century AD. All that remains of this house are cisterns, caverns, and a Jewish ritual bath called

Nazareth's Archaeological Layers

LAYER 6
Current church

LAYER 5
1730 church

LAYER 4
Crusader church

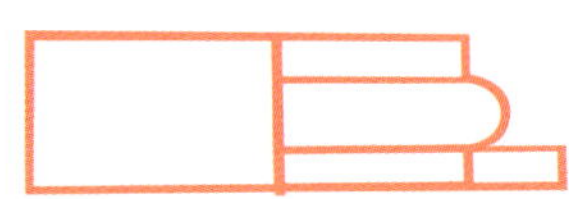

LAYER 3
Byzantine church

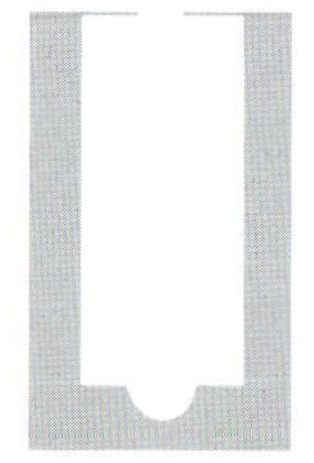

LAYER 2
Judeo-Christian synagogue (second century AD)

LAYER 1
Jewish ritual bath/ mikvah (time of Mary)

Img. 122: Key to the archaeological layers excavated at Nazareth.

a *mikvah* in Hebrew. One of the distinguishing features that enables an excavated house to be clearly identified as Jewish is finding a mikvah. For this particular house, the original mikvah was incorporated into a baptismal in the synagogue church that came after it.[8] Pottery and other finds from the level associated with the house established that it was occupied before, during, and after the first century AD.

The Bible tells us the event that occurred in this house over two thousand years ago, the event that over time transformed an ordinary house into the largest church in the Middle East.

> God sent the angel Gabriel to Nazareth, a town in Galilee, to a virgin pledged to be married to a man named Joseph, a descendant of David. The virgin's name was Mary. The angel went to her and said, "Greetings, you who are highly favored! The Lord is with you." Mary was greatly troubled at his words and wondered what kind of greeting this might be. But the angel said to her, "Do not be afraid, Mary; you have found favor with God. You will conceive and give birth to a son, and you are to call him Jesus. He will be great and will be called the Son of the Most High. The Lord God will give him the throne of his father David, and he will reign over Jacob's descendants forever; his kingdom will never end." "How will this be," Mary asked the angel, "since I am a virgin?" The angel answered, "The Holy Spirit will come on you, and the power of the Most High will overshadow you. So the holy one to be born will be called the Son of God." (Luke 1:26-35)

How do we know the authentic place where this earth-shattering announcement was made? Because of the phenomenon of building one thing on top of another. When the first archaeologist to excavate Nazareth arrived in 1892, there was no mystery at all concerning where to dig. The spot was clearly marked by a church named The Church of the Annunciation (Announcement)

THE INTERPRETATION

Gabriel had made the announcement of the ages. The offspring of Abraham, Isaac, and Jacob, the Lion of Judah and descendant of David was finally arriving. As a Jew, Mary expected the Messiah to come; she just didn't expect to conceive the Messiah. Because Mary was a descendant of David, he would be the Son of David; and, because he would be conceived by the Holy Spirit, he would be the Son of God, the eternal King. As Gabriel had announced, "[H]e will reign over Jacob's descendants forever; his kingdom will never end."

NOTES

1. Finegan, *The Archaeology of the New Testament*, 47–50. Finegan provides a good summary of the archaeological work in Nazareth.

2. Bellarmino Bagatti, *Excavations in Nazareth Volume 1: From Beginning Till the XII Century*, trans. Eugene Hoade (Jerusalem: Franciscan Printing Press, 1969), 6.

3. Ibid., See fig. 49 on p. 94 of Bagatti's excavation report for the plan showing what he found of the Byzantine church.

4. Bellarmino Bagatti, *The Church from the Circumcision: History and Archaeology of the Judeo-Christians*, Studium Biblicum Fransciscanum, Smaller Series (1984: repr., Jerusalem: Franciscan Printing Press, 1971), 125.

5. Ibid., 126–27.

6. Bagatti, *Excavations in Nazareth Volume 1*, 78.

7. Ibid.

8. Bagatti, *The Church from the Circumcision*, 125. See also Finegan, *Archaeology of the New Testament*, 47–54.

Chapter 7

THE SACRED CAVE

Bethlehem should be an obscure, unknown little village. Instead, the town receives visitors from all the nations, and its name is sung in carols around the world. Why? Because it was a landmark in God's redemptive plan.

Img. 123: Bethlehem, six miles south of Jerusalem.

Located on a mountain ridge in the old tribal area of Judah (Judges 17:7), six miles south of Jerusalem, Bethlehem was a relatively small village for most of its history—but in modern times, it has grown into a sizable Palestinian city.

For several years, I worked as a staff member in excavations at Bethlehem under an archaeologist, Dr. Shimon Gibson, and a historian, Dr. Joan Taylor. Though they would be considered secular in their beliefs, their interest in excavating Bethlehem stems from their understanding that the historical Jesus was born there. This understanding is not at odds with their respective fields, since the majority of scholars accept as historical the event that brought Bethlehem world fame. The question is, Why do they believe this? The answer is simple—evidence. The following is a discussion of the archaeological and historical evidence that confirms what we already knew from the New Testament—that the historical birthplace of Jesus Christ is indeed Bethlehem.

BETHLEHEM

Img. 124: This deep trench is part of the 2014–2015 excavation in Bethlehem.

Img. 125: A panorama of Bethlehem (red arrow identifying area of the ancient city) with Jerusalem in the far distance.

JERUSALEM

OLD TESTAMENT BETHLEHEM

In 1969 S. Gutman and A. Berman conducted an archaeological survey of the tel of Bethlehem. Their team systematically walked over a large area, collecting pottery from the surface of the ground. The pottery they found dated to the Iron Age II (1000–586 BC), Roman Period (63 BC–AD 324), and Byzantine Period (AD 324–638), establishing archaeologically that Bethlehem was occupied during these periods.[1]

The shaded area on the plan of Bethlehem (see *Img. 128*) shows where the survey team found Iron Age II pottery.[2] This gives us a basic outline of occupation, showing where Old Testament Bethlehem was located. In comparing the survey map with a recently-taken aerial photo (see *Img. 127*), we can see that the ancient tel of Bethlehem is now covered in houses and streets, which makes further excavation work challenging.

According to the evidence from the survey, on this hill and deep beneath the modern city is the town of Bethlehem, where long ago the following event took place:

> The Lord said to Samuel . . . "Fill your horn with oil and be on your way; I am sending you to Jesse of Bethlehem. I have chosen one of his sons to be king." Jesse had seven of his sons pass before Samuel, but Samuel said to him, "the Lord has not chosen these." So he asked Jesse, "Are these all the sons you have?" "There is still the youngest," Jesse answered. "He is tending the sheep." Samuel said, "Send for him; we will not sit down until he arrives." So he sent for him and had him brought in. He was glowing with health and had a fine appearance and handsome features. Then the Lord said, "Rise and anoint him; this is the one." So Samuel took the horn of oil and anointed him in the presence of his brothers, and from that day on the Spirit of the Lord came powerfully upon David. (1 Samuel 16:1, 10-13)

Toward the end of the eighth century BC, Micah prophesied that in the future the Messiah (which means Anointed One) would come from the same town where David had previously been anointed king.

> But as for you, Bethlehem Ephrathah, too little to be among the clans of Judah, from you One will go forth for Me to be ruler in Israel. His goings forth are from long ago, from the days of eternity. Therefore He will give them up until the time when she who is in labor has borne a child. (Micah 5:2-3 NASB)

From Bethlehem, the Anointed One (Messiah) would be born as a child. This remained the expectation in the first century AD. John's Gospel records a crowd of Jews saying, "Does not Scripture say that the Messiah will come from David's descendants and from Bethlehem, the town where David lived?" (John 7:42).

Img. 126: A photo of Dr. Shimon Gibson, archaeology professor and director of the excavation at the Church of the Nativity.

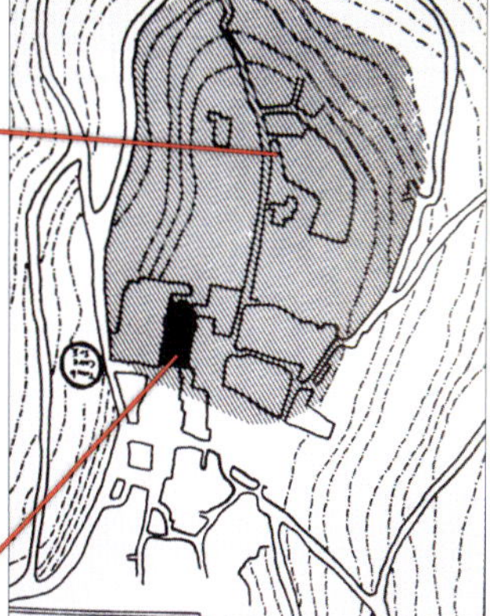

Img. 128: Survey plan of Bethlehem.

Img. 127: Aerial view of Bethlehem. The top red line identifies the highest point on the tel, while the lower red line correlates the location of the black building in the survey plan with its location in the aerial photo. The Bethlehem excavations revealed Iron Age II pottery dating from 1000 to 586 BC.

NEW TESTAMENT BETHLEHEM

Like the survey work of 1969 and previous excavations at Bethlehem, which we will discuss later, our excavation team also uncovered an abundance of pottery and other artifacts dating to the first century AD. Gibson explains the following in an interview I conducted with him:

> This is the Southwest corner of the Church of the Nativity. . . .We're sinking a trench down to early levels, and we have, without doubt, pottery dating from the time of Jesus. What we've been able to prove up until now is the existence of a village from the time of Jesus. This is very important.[3]

The Bethlehem we were excavating was where the following event occurred some two thousand years ago:

> So Joseph also went up from the town of Nazareth in Galilee to Judea, to Bethlehem the town of David, because he belonged to the house and line of David. He went there to register with Mary, who was pledged to be married to him and was expecting a child. While they were there, the time came for the baby to be born, and she gave birth to her firstborn, a son. She wrapped him in cloths and placed him in a manger, because there was no guest room available for them. (Luke 2:4-7)

In the hometown of King David was born the Son of David. David was a shepherd king, and so would be his offspring. The details of Jesus' birth paint that picture. The first contextual clue is that Jesus was laid in a manger. This detail implies that he was born among sheep since a manger, usually made of stone, is a trough used for watering and feeding sheep and other livestock.

Additionally, the text states that "there was no guest room available." This fits as there would not have been a manger inside a dwelling for people, only in a stable. Finally, not only was Jesus born

Img. 129: Excavations inside the Nativity Church in Bethlehem.

Img. 130: Excavations next to the Nativity Church in Bethlehem.

Img. 131: Aerial view of the Nativity Church in Bethlehem.

among sheep, but his birth was also announced to shepherds. The shepherds rejoiced and immediately set off to find him, but how would they know for certain which of the babies of Bethlehem was the Messiah? They were given a sign—he would be the baby lying in a manger. "So they hurried off and found Mary and Joseph, and the baby, who was lying in the manger" (Luke 2:16).

THE SACRED CAVE

When seeking out people to interview, I am always interested in hearing the perspectives of scholars who are not evangelical Christians. To hear a Jewish perspective on the longstanding Christian belief that Jesus was born in Bethlehem, I interviewed the well-known Israeli archaeologist, Dr. Gabriel Barkay.

BARKAY: Listen, I'm very objective, first of all; I'm an archaeologist and I'm not Christian.

JOEL: Where, personally, do you believe that Jesus was born?

BARKAY: Under the Church of the Nativity in Bethlehem there are some caves. And those cavities were in use in the first century beyond any doubt. For very important places, very significant places in Christian faith, I would regard the traditional places as authentic.[4]

The caves Barkay refers to were excavated in 1949–1950 by Bellarmino Bagatti, who found evidence establishing that they were in use in the first century AD.[5] One of these caves was described by Justin, who is known in church

Img. 132: Sheep and goats drinking from stone mangers in Israel.

history as Justin Martyr. As a well-traveled local of Judea, Justin wrote about Bethlehem in AD 150. His account is the earliest historical source for the birth of Jesus outside of the New Testament. "The Child was born in Bethlehem . . . in a certain cave ... there Mary brought forth the Christ and placed him in a manger." [6]

Img. 133: This is a typical stone manger in a sheep cave.

Justin records the added detail that Jesus was born in a cave, and there is no reason to doubt his statement since caves made ideal stables and therefore were common places to find mangers. Shepherd caves, as they are often called, provide sheep a place of refuge from heat and threat of predators. Since they remain cool in summer, warm in winter, and dry during the rainy season, sheep caves are often found beneath or beside ancient houses. Thus, Justin's early statement that Jesus was born in a cave fits well with the detail from Luke's Gospel that he was laid in a manger for watering and feeding sheep.

Img. 134: This photo, taken in 1934, shows a shepherd with his flock in a sheep cave. A cave provides ideal protection from the elements.

Img. 135: The entrance to a sheep cave is seen below the ruins of an old house. In the case of Jesus' birth, since there was no room in the house, Mary and Joseph stayed with the sheep in the cave, where, according to scripture, Jesus was born and then laid in a manger.

The early church historian Eusebius writes a similar account, saying "all agree" about where Jesus was born. He wrote around AD 313, "Now all agree that Jesus Christ was born in Bethlehem, and a cave is shewn there by the inhabitants to those who come from abroad to see it."[7]

Another person in antiquity who mentions Bethlehem in his writing is Origen. Living in Caesarea, Origen also visited Bethlehem, and writing in defense of Christianity in AD 248, he states the following:

> With respect to the birth of Jesus in Bethlehem, if any one desires, after the prophecy of Micah and after the history recorded in the Gospels by the disciples of Jesus, to have additional evidence from other sources, let him know that, in conformity with the narrative in the Gospel regarding His birth, there is shown at Bethlehem the cave where He was born, and the manger in the cave where He was wrapped in swaddling-clothes. And this sight is greatly talked of in surrounding places, even among the enemies of the faith, it being said that in this cave was born that Jesus who is worshiped and reverenced by the Christians.[8]

Origen presents the sacred cave as direct evidence for the birth of the Messiah, in agreement with the writings of Micah and the Gospels. He also points out that in his day, this sacred cave was known not only among Christians but also among "the enemies of the faith." Why would these enemies know about this cave? Another early historical source gives us the answer.

Jerome was a Christian priest who lived in the late fourth century. He moved to Bethlehem in order to learn Hebrew so he could translate the Old Testament into Latin. He was also a historian and gathered historical information from the locals. He wrote the following account in AD 395, describing Bethlehem as it had been after Emperor Hadrian's visit to the region in AD 130:

> From the time of Hadrian. . . . The original persecutors, indeed, supposed that by polluting our holy places they would deprive us of our faith. . . . Even my own Bethlehem . . . that most venerable spot in the whole world was overshadowed by a grove of Tammuz, that is of Adonis; and in the very cave where the infant Christ uttered His earliest cry lamentation was made for the paramour [lover] of Venus.[9]

This "polluting of holy places" should come as no surprise since the birthplace of Christ would have been an obvious target for Hadrian's overall plan to supplant Christian holy places with pagan ones. From the time of Hadrian to the time of Origen's writings in AD 248, Bethlehem's cave had already been used as a pagan worship place for more than a hundred years. This serves as yet another example of how even the desecration of a Christian holy place helped to preserve the memory of its authentic location.

THE CHURCH

When Constantine took control of the East, he reversed Hadrian's desecration and ordered a church to be built over the top of the holy cave, to once again commemorate the place in Bethlehem where Jesus Christ had been born. Eusebius's writings inform us of the constructions of this church around AD 327.[10] In AD 333 an unnamed pilgrim from Bordeaux who visited Bethlehem wrote, "There a basilica has been built by order of Constantine."[11]

Img. 136: Partial statue of Roman emperor Hadrian.

Img. 137: A statue of Jerome at the Church of the Nativity.

Constantine's original Church of the Nativity has been found and explored through archaeology, beginning with excavations by William Harvey in 1932 and 1934. Harvey unearthed enough of the walls, columns, and mosaic floors to provide an understanding of the building's structure. In his report, Harvey stated, "These discoveries . . . have revealed the great part of the plan [see *Img. 140*] of Constantine's Basilica."[12]

In the sixth century AD, Constantine's church was destroyed during a revolt against Emperor Justinian. It was soon rebuilt; and having undergone many repairs and restorations, this is the Church of the Nativity that visitors now experience in Bethlehem.

Serving as a marker of authenticity, the current church has stood for some fifteen centuries over the sacred cave where Jesus Christ was born more than two thousand years ago.

Dr. Joan Taylor, historian and co-director of the archaeology dig at the Church of the Nativity, drew the following conclusion from her excavations and research:

> The Church of the Nativity is built on the site traditionally where Jesus was born. Historically it's got really good credibility as being the place where Jesus' family lived, and he was born right here.[13]

Although Jewish, Christian, and secular scholars may hold different beliefs about who Jesus was, the vast majority agree that He was a historical person who was born in Bethlehem. The textual and archaeological evidence places the birthplace of Jesus at Bethlehem into the category of historical fact.

Img. 138: This shows the Constantinian mosaic floor as it appears today after restoration.

Img. 139: A 1934 photo of the floor of Constantine's original church, revealed through William Harvey's excavations.

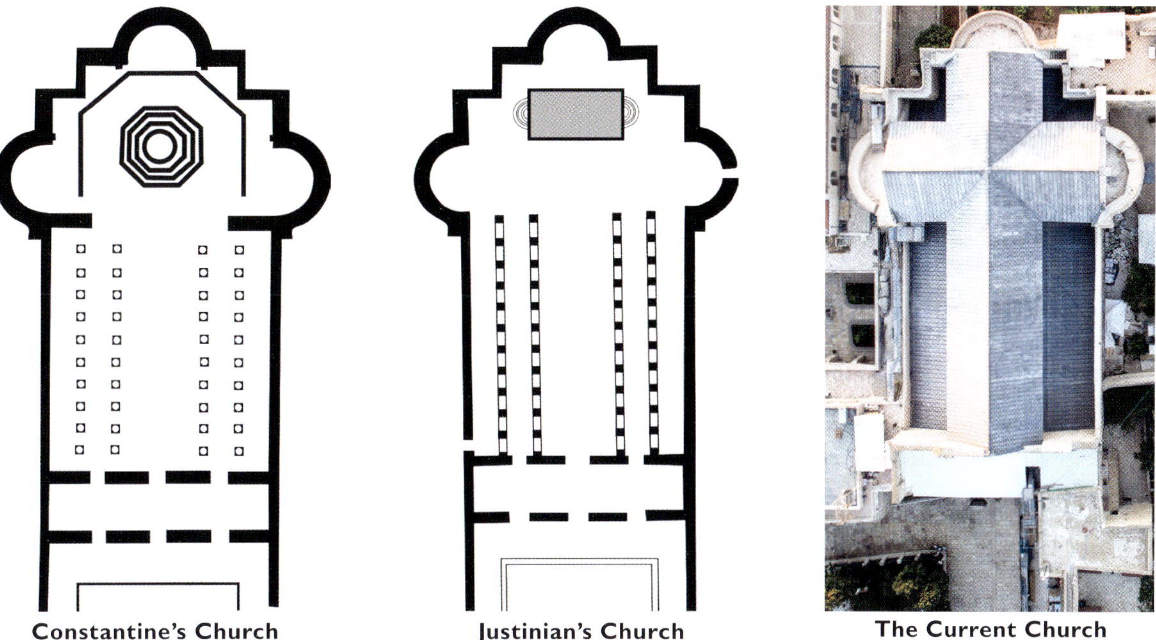

Img. 140: These are side-by-side plan views of Constantine's, Justinian's, and the current church.

Img. 141: A typical shepherd's cave.

Img. 142: A shepherd's cave beneath the Church of the Nativity.

Img. 143: The Nativity cave beneath the apse of the church, next to the cave shown in Img. 142.

Img. 144: The star represents the place of Jesus' birth.

THE INTERPRETATION

Matthew's Gospel tells us about another event that took place at some point after Jesus' birth:

> After Jesus was born in Bethlehem in Judea, during the time of King Herod, Magi from the east came to Jerusalem and asked, "Where is the one who has been born king of the Jews? We saw his star when it rose and have come to worship him." When King Herod heard this he was disturbed, and all Jerusalem with him. When he had called together all the people's chief priests and teachers of the law, he asked them where the Messiah was to be born. "In Bethlehem in Judea," they replied, "for this is what the prophet has written: 'But you, Bethlehem, in the land of Judah, are by no means least among the rulers of Judah: for out of you will come a ruler who will shepherd my people Israel.'" (Matthew 2:1-6)

Herod wanted to know "where the Messiah was to be born," and Micah's prophecy, given around seven centuries before this event, gave him the answer: "In Bethlehem in Judea." Micah's prophecy also predicted of the Messiah that "He [would be] great to the ends of the earth" (Micah 5:4 NASB). Who is known throughout the world more than Jesus Christ? At the very least, Jesus is one of the most famous persons in all of human history. There is no real reason that a poor Jewish man, born in a cave in Bethlehem, should have been known by anyone outside of his own village and his own time. And yet, knowledge of Jesus has continued to spread throughout the world for the past two thousand years. Billions of people from all nations of the world have come to believe in Jesus as their Messiah. His followers still visit the cave where He was born more than two thousand years ago. In the scope of human history, who else was born in Bethlehem of Judea and is known "to the ends of the earth"? Micah's eighth-century-BC prophecy proved correct.

Since no man knows the future (Ecclesiastes 8:7), only God can tell us what the future holds. The fact that the Bible identified where the Messiah

Img. 145: After almost 35 years of excavating the Herodium, Israeli archaeologist Ehud Netzer finally found Herod the Great's mausoleum and long-buried sarcophagus in 2007.

Img. 146: This is an old photograph of pilgrims from all over the world, visiting Bethlehem as they have done for thousands of years and continue today.

Img. 147: From the hills in the distance, Bethlehem looks down on the Herodium.

would be born before His birth points to the reality that the Bible is historical *and* authoritative.

Another detail in Micah's prophecy is that the one who would come from Bethlehem would also come "from the days of eternity" (Micah 5:2 NASB). Only God could come from eternity. The Messiah would be both man and God. This God-child is the one the magi went to Bethlehem to seek.

> After they [the magi] had heard the king, they went on their way, and the star they had seen when it rose went ahead of them until it stopped over the place where the child was. When they saw the star, they were overjoyed. On coming to the house, they saw the child with his mother Mary, and they bowed down and worshiped him. (Matthew 2:9-11)

Jesus was not only born in Bethlehem, but He was also worshiped there. Jesus was central to God's redemptive plan, which is why His birthplace became a pivotal battleground for the souls of mankind. Through John's revelation, we see war raging in the heavenly realm, far beyond the earthly nativity scene:

> A great sign appeared in heaven: a woman clothed with the sun, with the moon under her feet and a crown of twelve stars on her head. She was pregnant and cried out in pain as she was about to give birth. Then another sign appeared in heaven: an enormous red dragon with seven heads and ten horns and seven crowns on its heads. Its tail swept a third of the stars out of the sky and flung them to the earth. The dragon stood in front of the woman who was about to give birth, so that it might devour her child the moment he was born. She gave birth to a son, a male child, who "will rule all the nations with an iron scepter." Then I heard a loud voice in heaven say: "Now have come the salvation and the power and the kingdom of our God, and the authority of his Messiah." (Revelation 12:1-5, 10)

Glimpsing the heavenly scene helps us to understand the earthly stage. Herod the Great is acting on behalf of the dragon, attempting to kill the dragon's nemesis.

> An angel of the Lord appeared to Joseph in a dream. "Get up," he said, "take the child and his mother and escape to Egypt. Stay there until I tell you, for Herod is going to search for the child to kill him." When Herod realized that he had been outwitted by the Magi, he was furious, and gave orders to kill all the boys in Bethlehem and its vicinity who were two years old and under. (Matthew 2:13, 16)

Herod failed. The dragon failed. The child escaped—and lived.

Before we finish our examination of Bethlehem, we must answer one final question: Why did God need to be born as a human baby? The answer lies in the announcement of Jesus' birth given to the shepherds. Angels declared the child's purpose, saying, "Today in the town of David a Savior has been born to you" (Luke 2:11). So how exactly does God being born human save us?

Like Isaac on Mount Moriah, what mankind needed was a substitute sacrifice. Sinful man needed someone sinless to die in his place. God is sinless, eternal, immortal, and indestructible, and He cannot die. So in order to save the world, God had to take for Himself a human body that was capable of dying. Jesus was born in order to die ... and yet, three days after He died, He would rise from the dead.

Img. 148: This is an aerial view of Bethlehem, looking south over the Church of the Nativity.

Img. 149: A shepherd tends his flock in a field with Bethlehem in the background.

NOTES

1. S. Gutman and A. Berman, "Chronique Archéologique," *Revue Biblique* 77 (1970): 583–85.

2. Ibid., fig. 3, 584. For more Iron Age pottery evidence found at Bethlehem see Sylvester Saller, "Iron Age Remains from the Site of a New School at Bethlehem," *Liber Annus* 18 (1968): 153–80.

3. This quote is from my personal interview with Dr. Shimon Gibson can be seen at: sourceflix.com/our-video/born-in-bethlehem/.

4. Joel P. Kramer, *The Bible vs. Joseph Smith*, DVD, (www.sourceflix.com, 2010).

5. Bellarmino Bagatti, *Gli Antichi Edifici Sacri Di Betlemme in Seguito Agli Scavi E Restauri Praticati Dalla Custodia Di Terra Santa (1948–51) PSBF 9* (Jerusalem: Franciscan Printing Press, 1952). See also Bellarmino Bagatti and Eugene Hoade, *The Church of the Gentiles in Palestine: History and Archaeology* (Jerusalem: Franciscan Printing Press, 1971), 175–84.

6. Justin Martyr, "Dialogue of Justin with Trypho, a Jew," 1:237.

7. Eusebius, *The Proof of the Gospel*, 1:112.

8. Origen, "Origen against Celsus," in *Fathers of the Third Century: Tertullian, Part Fourth; Minucius Felix; Commodian; Origen, Parts First and Second,* eds. Alexander Roberts, James Donaldson, and A. Cleveland Coxe, trans. Frederick Crombie, vol. 4, The Ante-Nicene Fathers. (Buffalo, New York: The Christian Literature Publishing Company, 1885), 418.

9. Jerome, *St. Jerome: Letters and Select Works*, eds. Philip Schaff and Henry Wallace, A Select Library of the Nicene and Post–Nicene Fathers of the Christian Church, Second Series, vol. 6 (New York: Christian Literature Company, 1893), 120.

10. Eusebius, *The Life of the Blessed Emperor Constantine*, 147-48.

11. Finegan, *The Archaeology of the New Testament*, 31.

12. William Harvey, *Structural Survey of the Church of the Nativity, Bethlehem* (London: Oxford University Press, H. Milford, 1935), 30. For reconstructions see also Hugues Vincent and F. M. Abel, *Bethléem, Le Sanctuaire De La Nativité*, ed. J. Gabalda (Paris: Librairie Victor Lecoffre, 1914).

13. This quote is from my personal interview with Dr. Joan Taylor of King's College London and can be seen at: sourceflix.com/our-video/born-in-bethlehem/.

Chapter 8

THE GARDEN

The most established historical event associated with Jesus of Nazareth is His crucifixion. In addition to early, independent sources in the New Testament, there are also well-known extra-biblical sources that document His death. The first century AD Jewish historian Josephus wrote, "At this time there was a wise man called Jesus … Pilate condemned him to be crucified and to die."[1] Tacitus, another Roman historian writing after Josephus, explained, "Christus from whom the name [Christian] had its origin, suffered the extreme penalty during the reign of Tiberius at the hands of one of our procurators, Pontius Pilatus."[2] Additionally, Jewish rabbis remembered this event: "Jesus of Nazareth was hanged on Passover Eve."[3]

Img. 150: This tomb, with a rolling stone and kokhim (burial niches), was discovered in Nazareth and dates to the time of Jesus.

Since the fact of Jesus' crucifixion is so well established, we will move forward to examine the evidence surrounding where His crucifixion and burial took place.

Img. 151: The two kokhim in the garden in Jerusalem were already visible before Corbo excavated.

TIME OF JESUS (AD 33)

Excavations carried out by archaeologist Virgilio Corbo in Jerusalem from the early 1960s through the early 1980s unearthed an ancient garden that had been used as a place to cultivate grapes, figs, and olives.[4] Preserved within the garden were two small burial niches called *kokhim* which can still be seen today. Kokhim were used in Jewish burial practices exclusively at the end of the first century BC and into the first century AD. Finding them in this garden provides incontrovertible evidence that it had been in use as a Jewish cemetery at the time of Christ's crucifixion and burial.

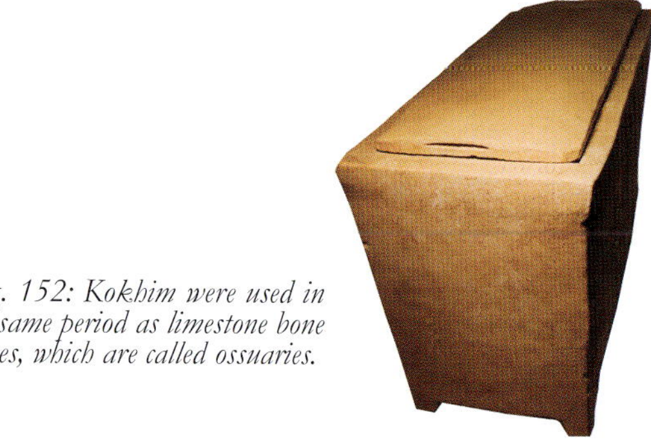
Img. 152: Kokhim were used in the same period as limestone bone boxes, which are called ossuaries.

Excavating in Jerusalem in the early 1970s, archaeologist Nahman Avigad discovered the remains of a Roman-Period city gate. He identified it as the Gennath Gate.[5] Josephus wrote of the gate, "The second wall took its beginning from that gate which they called 'Gennath,' which belonged to the first wall."[6]

Img. 153: An authentic Jewish tomb from the time of Jesus. After a corpse was placed in the tomb, the massive rolling stone was rolled into place to seal it. An angel sat on the rolling stone that sealed Jesus' tomb, waiting to announce His resurrection.

When translated, *Gennath Gate* means "Garden Gate."[7] The road coming out from the Gennath Gate passed just to the east of the ancient garden Corbo excavated. Logically, then, this was the garden from which the Garden (Gennath) Gate derived its name.

Because Jews considered tombs unclean, burial sites or cemeteries were not allowed inside the city walls.[8] It follows that Corbo's ancient garden containing first century tombs had to have been located outside the city walls, just beyond the Garden Gate. This idea concurs with the biblical account of the crucifixion and burial of Jesus: "And so Jesus also suffered *outside the city gate* to make the people holy through his own blood" (Hebrews 13:12; emphasis added).

It is also important to understand that other than a short window of time during the AD 70 destruction, Christians continually lived in Jerusalem—from the time of Jesus to the present. Even over the course of many years, the location of events as significant as Christ's death and resurrection would not have been forgotten by Jesus' followers or even by the rest of the local population. Instead, the locations were marked and commemorated by Christians and even pagans, although for other reasons. Searching layer by layer, archaeologists can identify these two sites through time.

TIME OF HADRIAN (Beginning AD 130)

In the same excavation, Virgilio Corbo unearthed several foundation walls dating to the Late Roman Period. Additionally, Corbo found various cultic artifacts, including an altar for burning incense.[9] These finds were evidence that Hadrian had done the same thing in Jerusalem he had done at Mamre and Bethlehem—that is, built his own worship sites over existing Christian holy sites. In Jerusalem (called Aelia Capitolina at that time) Hadrian desecrated Christianity's two most holy sites: Golgotha, the place of Jesus' crucifixion, and

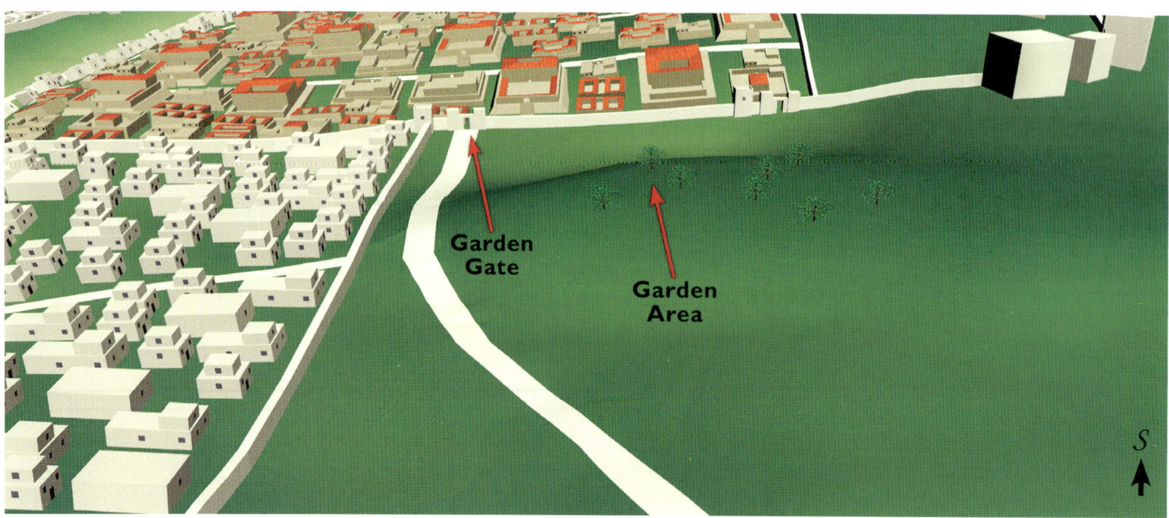

Img. 154: Red arrow indicates where the garden would have been located, outside and to the west of the Garden Gate.

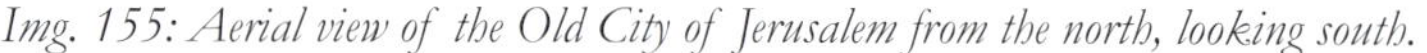

Img. 155: Aerial view of the Old City of Jerusalem from the north, looking south.

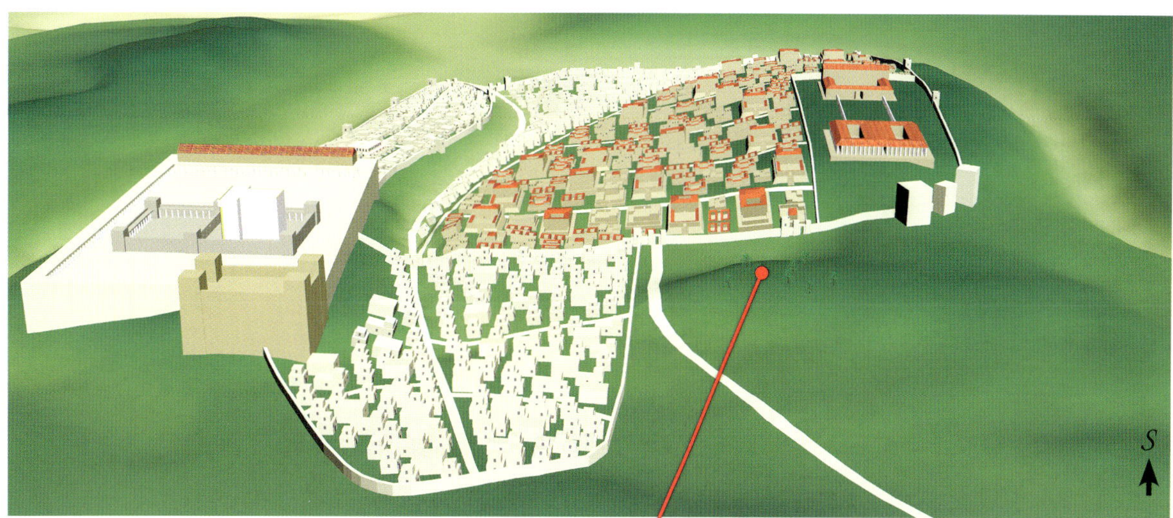

Img. 156: In this reconstruction of Jerusalem at the time of Jesus, west of the Garden Gate (discovered by Nahman Avgad). The red line correlates the area of the garden to where it would be located in the Old City of Jerusalem today.

Jesus' burial tomb, the place of His resurrection. The Apostle John described the two sites:

> *At the place* where Jesus was crucified, *there was a garden*, and *in the garden* a new tomb, in which no one had ever been laid. Because it was the Jewish day of Preparation and since *the tomb was nearby*, they laid Jesus there. (John 19:41-42; emphasis added)

Since these two venerated sites were "nearby," Hadrian was able to construct a temple platform over both of them together. The first stage was to build up a foundation. Eusebius describes the work:

> Accordingly they [the Romans] brought a quantity of earth from a distance with much labor, and covered the entire spot [by burying it]; then, having raised this to a moderate height, they paved it with stone.[10]

Like the walls bounding Mount Moriah, foundation walls were built around the perimeter of the garden area, creating a stone box of sorts. Next, those walls were filled in with dirt that was packed down and paved with stones to create a flat platform on which to build. The walls of this foundation, which Corbo found in his excavations, were the walls that surrounded Golgotha and the tomb.

The writings of early church father Jerome give more details about what rose up on Hadrian's paved-over platform:

> From the time of Hadrian to the reign of Constantine—a period of about one hundred and eighty years—the spot which had witnessed the resurrection was occupied by a figure of Jupiter; while on the rock where the cross had stood, a marble statue of Venus was set up by the heathen and became an object of worship. The original persecutors, indeed, supposed that by polluting our holy places they would deprive us of our faith in the passion and in the resurrection.[11]

That there were two statues may be an indication that Hadrian had constructed two temples, one for Jupiter and another for Venus. It is also possible that a single temple housed both statues, as Hadrian also built a double temple of this style in Rome for the god Roma and the goddess Venus.

Regardless of the style of the temple(s), what is important to understand is that it was no mystery for Christians living there at the time to know where

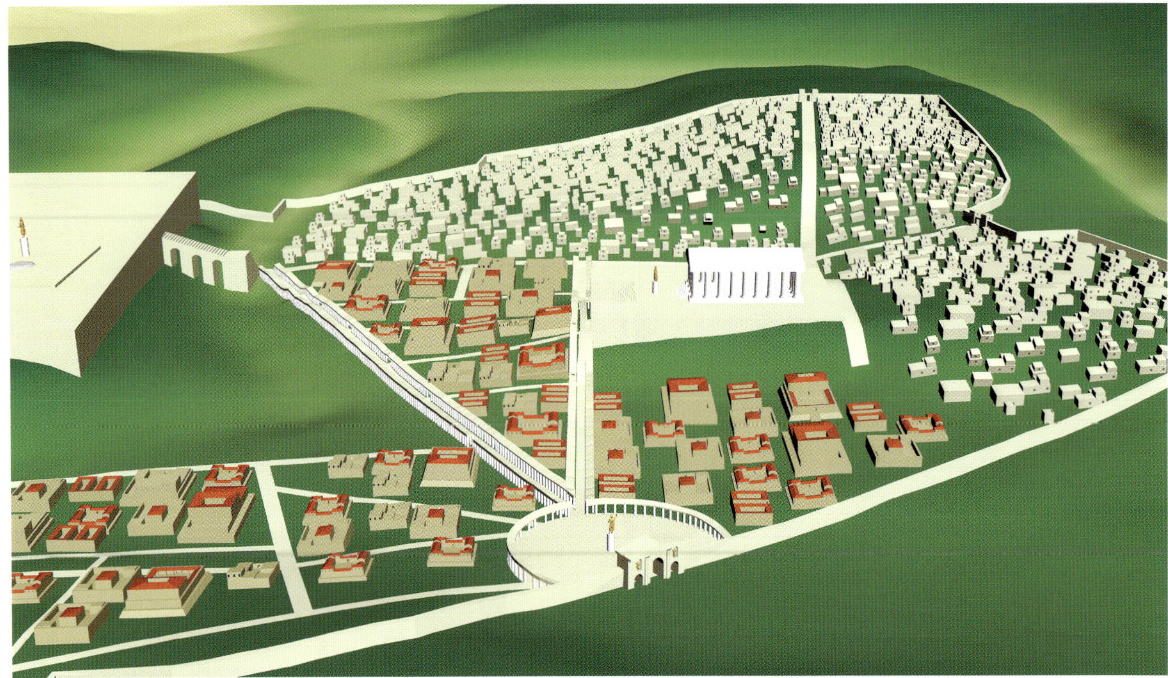

Img. 157: Reconstruction of Aelia Capitolina, the city which Hadrian constructed over the rubble from the AD 70 Roman destruction of Jerusalem. The focal place for Hadrian's new city was the main temple, which he built over Jesus' crucifixion and burial sites.

their Savior died, was buried, and rose again. There were two huge pagan statues marking the spots.

TIME OF CONSTANTINE (AD 324)

After a number of years of co-ruling, Emperor Constantine eventually took sole control of the eastern portion of the Roman Empire. As his biographer, Eusebius offers an eyewitness description of how paganism fell in Aelia Capitolina, after almost two hundred years, once Constantine came to power:

> As soon, then, as his [Constantine's] commands were issued, these engines of deceit were cast down from their proud eminence to the very ground, and the dwelling-places of error, with the statues and the evil spirits which they represented, were overthrown and utterly destroyed. Nor did the emperor's zeal stop here; but he gave further orders that the materials of what was thus destroyed, both stone and timber, should be removed and thrown as far from the spot as possible; and this command also was speedily executed.[12]

As the emperor of Rome, only Constantine had the authority to order the destruction of Aelia Capitolina's main temple while it was still in full use. He did give those orders; the temple was destroyed and removed, just as Eusebius described.

With the temple gone, Eusebius also records what came next: the first recorded archaeological dig in Jerusalem (Aelia Capitolina) commenced under the supervision of Macarius, Bishop of Jerusalem. Although this excavation took place almost fifteen centuries before archaeology would become an academic field, the goal of this endeavor was archaeological in nature. Its purpose: to unearth the holy sites of Christ. How did Macarius know where to dig for Christianity's buried holy places? The answer was obvious—beneath the temple where pagan statues had stood. Eusebius explains:

> The emperor, however, was not satisfied with having proceeded thus far: once more, fired with holy ardour, he

Img. 158: A coin, front and back, minted by Hadrian. His bust is on the front side (above, left), and on the reverse side (above, right) is a man plowing with oxen to lay out the boundaries for the new city which Hadrian planned to build on top of the plowed ruins of Jerusalem. The name of Hadrian's new city also appears on the upper right of the back of the coin—"Aelia."

Img. 159: A coin depicting the main temple which Hadrian directed to be built in Aelia Capitolina. This temple was adorned with a statue of Jupiter and Venus.

Img. 160: Entry way, steps, and a wall line leading up to the temple Hadrian built on top of Golgotha.

> directed that the ground itself should be dug up to a considerable depth, and the soil which had been polluted by the foul impurities of demon worship transported to a far distant place.
>
> This also was accomplished without delay. But as soon as the original surface of the ground, beneath the covering of earth, appeared, immediately . . . the venerable and hallowed monument of our Saviour's resurrection was discovered. Then indeed did this most holy cave [tomb] present a faithful similitude of His return to life, in that, after lying buried in darkness, it again emerged to light, and afforded to all who came to witness the sight, a clear and visible proof of the wonders of which that spot had once been the scene, a testimony to the resurrection of the Saviour clearer than any voice could give.[13]

The place of Jesus' resurrection had been unearthed, and at the same time the place of crucifixion was also uncovered just to the east of the sacred tomb. Many archaeological excavations have taken place in Jerusalem since, but none have come close to equaling that initial effort which unearthed Jesus' tomb and Golgotha.

Once the holy sites were unburied, Constantine again issued orders—this time not to destroy, however, but to build. He ordered that a church be erected over the sites to protect and commemorate them.

During excavations in 1968, archaeologist Athanase Economopolous discovered the apse of a church that he identified as belonging to the commemorative church built by Constantine over Golgotha.[14] The church's apse marked the spot of crucifixion and faced west, pointing toward the tomb of Jesus. Enough of its structure was uncovered to enable a drawn reconstruction of the overall architecture (see *Img. 163*).

Eusebius recounts the building of the church:

> Accordingly, on the very spot which witnessed the Saviour's sufferings, a new Jerusalem was constructed . . . For at the side opposite to the sepulchre [Jesus' tomb], which was the eastern side, the church itself was erected; a noble work rising to a vast height, and of great extent both in length and breadth.[15]

This church was called the Martyrium, a Greek word from which the English word martyr is derived. Constantine spared no expense in adorning it as the crown of all churches. He instructed in a letter,

> It will be well, therefore, for you Sagacity to make such arrangements and provisions of all things needful for the work, that not only the church itself as a whole may surpass all others whatsoever in beauty, but that the details of the building may be of such a kind that the fairest structures in any city of the empire may be excelled by this.[16]

West of the Martyrium church, Constantine had a mausoleum constructed over the tomb of Jesus. This circular structure called the Anastasis, "resurrection" in Greek, was built in the imperial style of the day, with walls and pillars surrounding the tomb of Jesus. Mausoleums were elaborate monuments, often freestanding, built

Img. 161 and Img. 162: Emperor Constantine ordered Hadrian's Temple (above) to be destroyed. He then commissioned the construction of a church (below) to commemorate the crucifixion site, Golgotha, and a mausoleum to be built over Jesus' tomb. Once again, we can see the phenomenon of "one thing built on top of another."

to house the tombs and remains of important figures, such as the emperors of Rome. It would have seemed fitting for Constantine to house the empty tomb of the King of Kings in the style of a royal mausoleum. A patch of the western side of the mausoleum housing is still preserved.[17]

Eusebius described Constantine's orders regarding the lavish mausoleum he built:

> There upon the emperor issued sacred edicts and, when he had provided an abundant supply of all the things required for the project, he gave orders that a house of prayer worthy of God should be erected round about the Cave [Tomb] of Salvation, and on a scale of rich and imperial costliness.[18]

The account of the unnamed pilgrim from Bordeaux in AD 333 provides the following description of these buildings:

> On your left is the little hill of Golgotha where the Lord was crucified. About a stone's throw from it is the crypt where they laid his body, and [from where he] rose again on the third day. These are present, by order of Constantine, there has been built a 'basilica,' that is, a church of wondrous beauty.[19]

Another pilgrim named Egeria provides an inside view of the Anastasis and Martyrium in a service she attended there in AD 380:

> I know you are eager to know about the services they have daily in the holy places, I shall tell you about them … when the first cock has crowed, the bishop straightaway enters and goes into the cave [tomb] in the Anastasis, and the whole crowd streams into the Anastasis, which is already ablaze with many lamps. … Then the bishop, standing inside the screen, takes the Gospel and advances to the door [of the tomb], where he himself reads the account of the Lord's Resurrection. … When the Gospel is finished, the bishop comes out and is taken with hymns to the Cross, and they all go with him … they go to the Great Church, the Martyrium … the people assemble in the Great Church built by Constantine on Golgotha.[20]

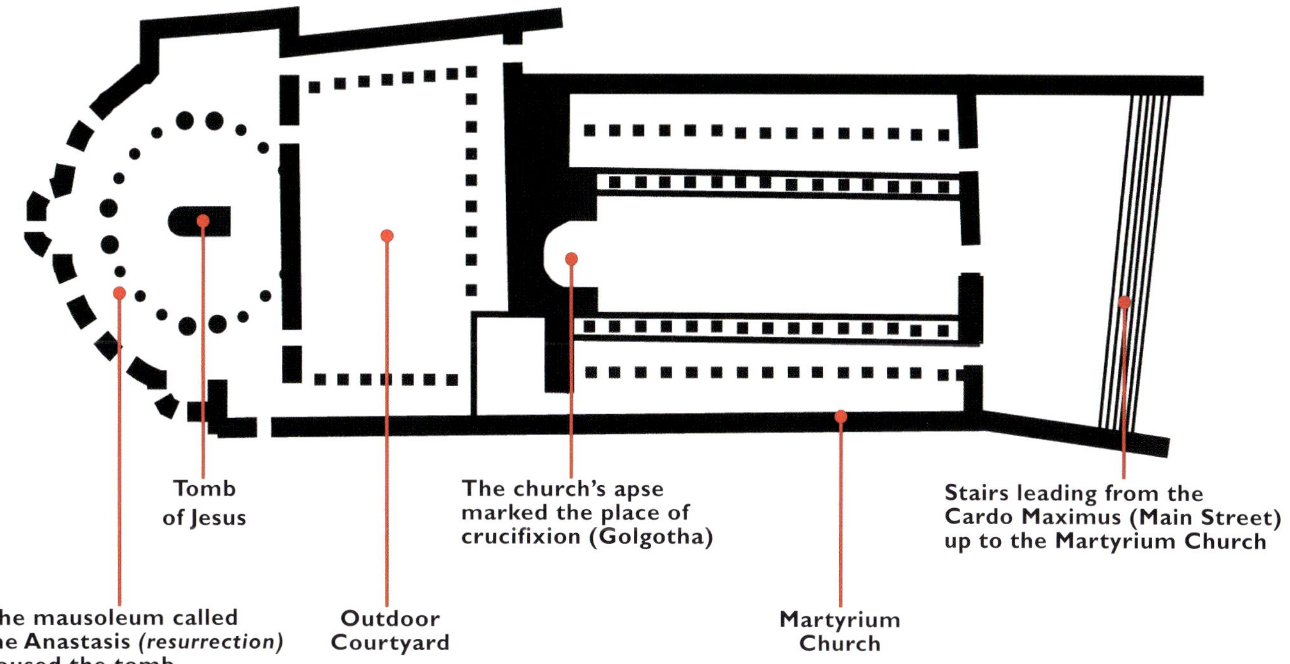

Img. 163: Enough evidence was preserved from these earlier structures to provide a plan of Constantine's original buildings.

TIME OF CONSTANTINE

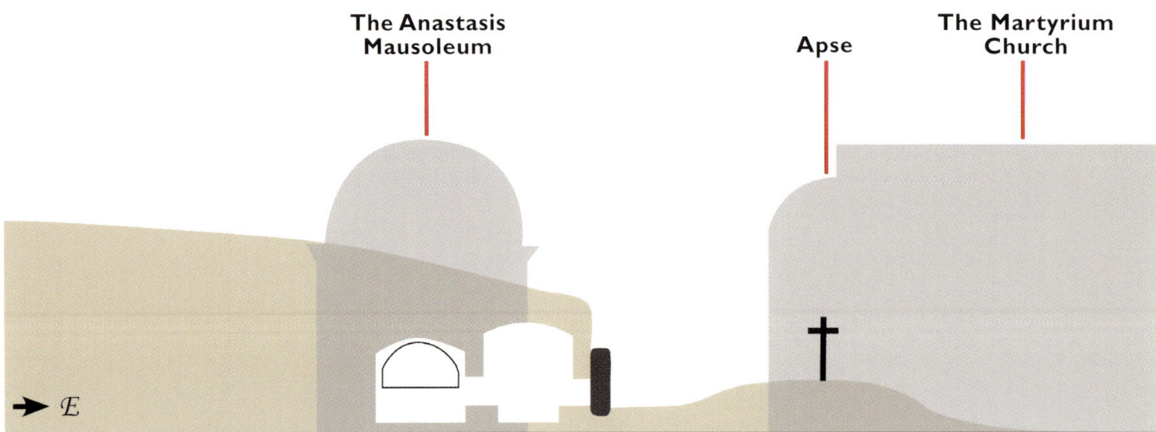

HADRIAN'S TEMPLE

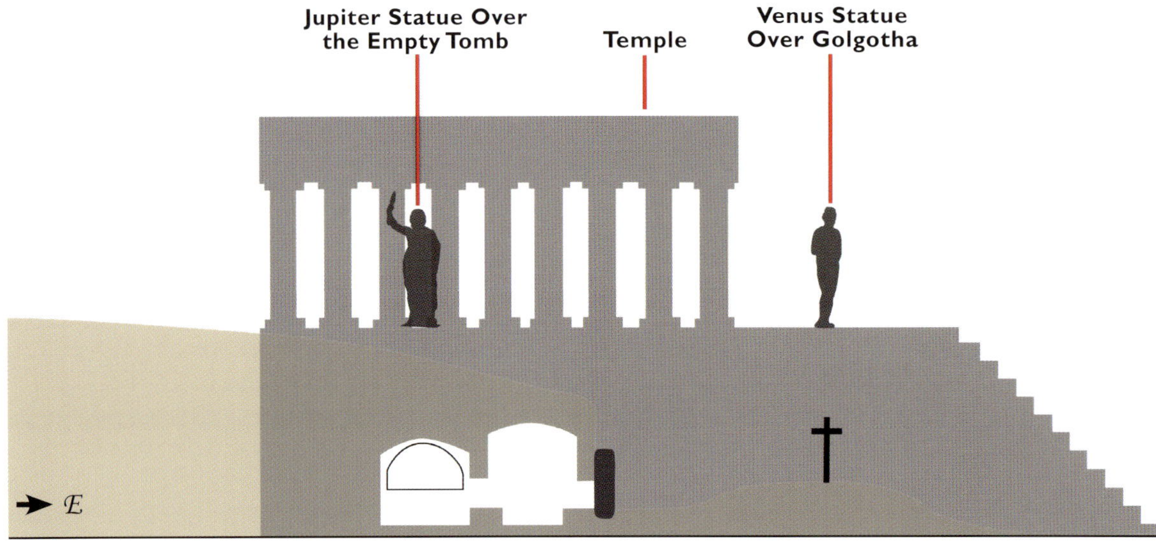

TIME OF JESUS

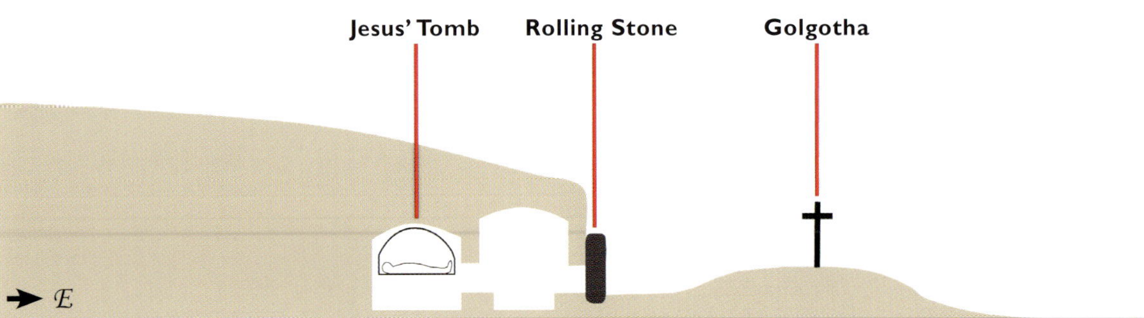

Img. 164: These three graphics illustrate the progressive layers as they were constructed over the crucifixion and burial site by Hadrian and then by Constantine.

Amazingly, we have a picture of these buildings preserved in a mosaic in the Church of Santa Pudenziana in Rome (see *Img. 166*). This mosaic in the church's apse is the oldest known image of Jerusalem and dates to about AD 400. In the center of the mosaic (see *Img. 167*), Jesus Christ sits on a throne. Behind and to the left of him are two buildings. The mausoleum housing Jesus' tomb, the Anastasis, is the circular building with a dome. Behind the Anastasis, to the east, is the Martyrium church, built over the site of Golgotha, also called Calvary, where Jesus was crucified.

FROM CONSTANTINE TO PRESENT

The Anastasis and Martyrium were destroyed by fire during the Persian invasion in AD 614. Though quickly rebuilt, they were destroyed again by Islamic invaders in AD 1009.[21]

After several cycles of destruction, crusaders constructed another church in the mid-twelfth century. This church, the Church of the Holy Sepulchre, is currently visible to us. It sits atop the two sacred sites, and its two grey domes are the markers we can see today, identifying where Jesus died and rose again.

Sadly, there is little left of Jesus' tomb today, having suffered destruction at the hands of enemies who tried to desecrate it as well as adoring pilgrims who chipped away little pieces to carry home with them.

The authenticity of Golgotha and Jesus' tomb, like other sites previously covered, can be verified by layers of archaeological remains, one thing on top of another, and through credible historical sources that describe what happened there. Both the archaeological evidence and the historical evidence originate from multiple periods, covering the span of time from the original sacred events in the first century AD to the present.

The evidence available to us to authenticate these two sacred sites is overwhelming. We can be sure that the Church of the Holy Sepulchre, standing today in the Old City of Jerusalem, marks the place where Jesus died and where He rose again.

THE INTERPRETATION

The Bible tells us about two gardens: the Garden of Eden and a garden in Jerusalem. Eden's garden held perfection and newly-created life. Jerusalem's garden held Golgotha and a freshly-cut tomb. These two gardens are the stages upon which the critical plot line of the story of mankind's relationship with God played out. In the first garden, man disobeyed, sin entered, death came, and God's relationship with mankind was broken. In the second garden, the Son of Man obeyed, sin was paid for, death was destroyed, and a way for relationship with God was restored.

We can see this brokenness and restoration in the story of the two criminals who died along with Jesus in the garden at Golgotha:

> One of the criminals who hung there hurled insults at him: "Aren't you the Messiah? Save yourself and us!" But the other criminal rebuked him. "Don't you fear God," he said, "since you are under the same sentence? We are punished justly, for we are getting what our deeds deserve. But this man has done nothing wrong." Then he said, "Jesus, remember me when you come into your kingdom." Jesus answered him, "Truly I tell you, today you will be with me in paradise." (Luke 23:39-43)

The first criminal failed to recognize that God Himself was hanging next to him, willing to pay

Img. 165: The Church of Santa Pudenziana in Rome contains an amazing mosaic of the city of Jerusalem in the Byzantine Period.

Img. 166: A mosaic in the apse of the Church of Santa Pudenziana, a basilica in Rome, incorporates an early, detailed image of Jerusalem dating to about AD 400 when the church was built.

Img. 167: An amazingly preserved mosaic picture, over 1,600 years old, of the structures built by Constantine, commemorating the death and resurrection of Jesus Christ.

CHURCH OF THE HOLY SEPULCHRE

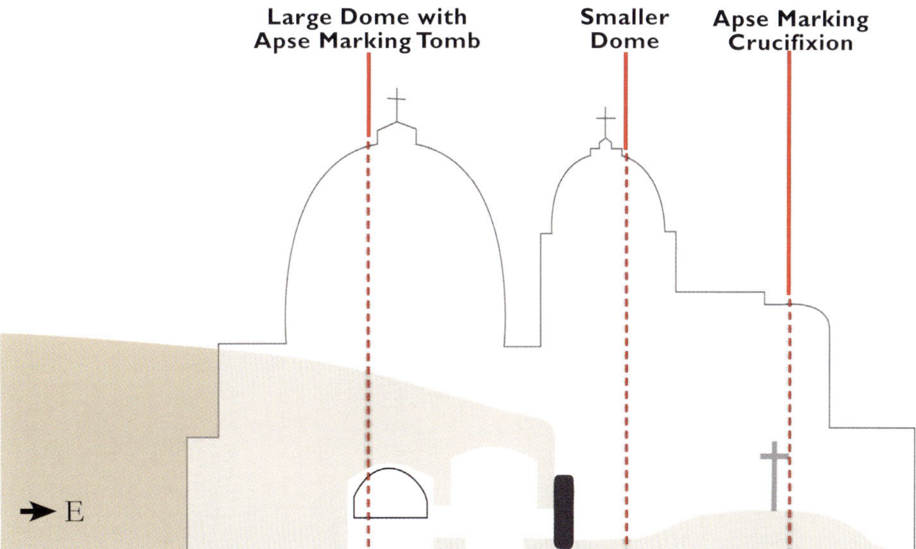

Img. 168: This graphic illustrates the orientation of the present-day Church of the Holy Sepulchre over Golgotha and the tomb of Jesus.

Img. 169: An aerial view of the Church of the Holy Sepulchre. The red arrow points to the apse of the church, which marks the place of crucifixion. The larger dome on the far left marks the location of the tomb of Jesus and his resurrection.

Img. 170: An aerial view of the Holy Sepulchre's three east-facing apses. (note direction arrow, bottom left corner).

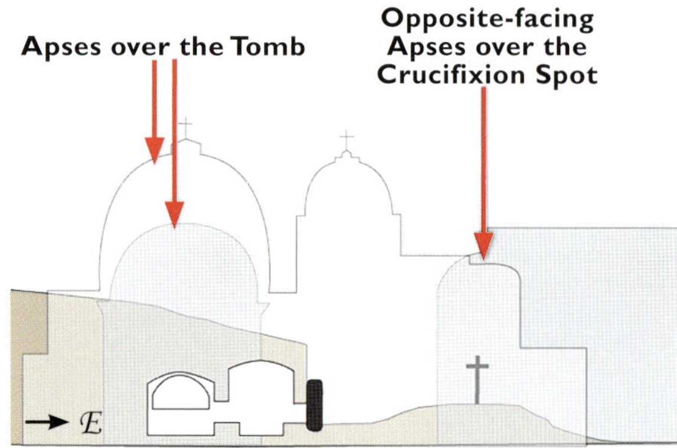

Img. 171: Though facing opposite directions, both apses line up over the same spot, identifying and commemorating it as Golgotha.

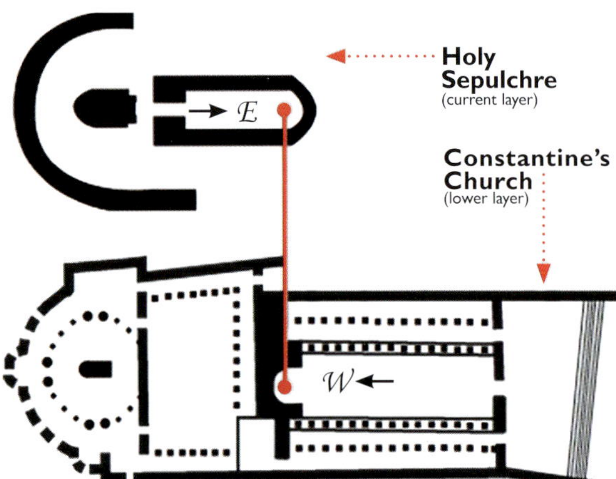

Img. 172: Plans for the Holy Sepulchre and the original Constantinian church. Note each of the apses marking the crucifixion face in opposite directions: the apse of the Holy Sepulchre faces east, while the apse of the original church faces west. Imagine these plans stacked on top of each other to get the proper orientation.

Img. 173: Today's visitors to the Holy Sepulchre are directed to the crucifixion spot, reached by climbing very narrow stairs just inside the church. However, the far older tradition that marks Golgotha's location is identifiable by the placement of the church's apse. This picture is looking through a gap, down onto the center of the apse.

Img. 174: A tomb from the first century AD. Jesus' tomb would have been similar to this one. The destruction from both enemies and pilgrims necessitated building a structure to preserve the location of the tomb.

Img. 175: A picture from 1941 of worshipers from all over the world, surrounding the tomb of Jesus. The actual tomb suffered extreme damage in antiquity. Each time an enemy destroyed the church, they also destroyed what the church commemorated—the tomb. To protect what remained of the tomb, an edicule (the structure in the middle of the picture) was built around it. A new edicule was constructed in 2017.

Img. 176: This graphic illustration shows all of the architectural layers (superimposed one on top of another) that have been built over Christianity's two holiest places. These two buildings were built to commemorate, or in the case of Hadrian to desecrate, the crucifixion site and the burial and resurrection site.

Img. 177: In the above picture, Jews are visiting the grave of a rabbi on the Mount of Olives, across the Kidron Valley from the Old City of Jerusalem. Just as Jews today visit the graves of their rabbis, so the early followers of Jesus visited the tomb where their Rabbi was buried and raised from the dead. Believers in Jesus have been visiting His tomb ever since His resurrection; because, with the exception of a brief time at the AD 70 destruction, Christians have lived in Jerusalem continually from the days of Jesus until today.

Img. 178: Christians gathered at the Holy Sepulchre in 1898.

Img. 179: A reconstruction of Jerusalem at the time of Jesus.

Img. 180: Looking from the same angle (as Img. 179), this reconstruction shows how much the city changed as Hadrian built up Aelia Capitolina.

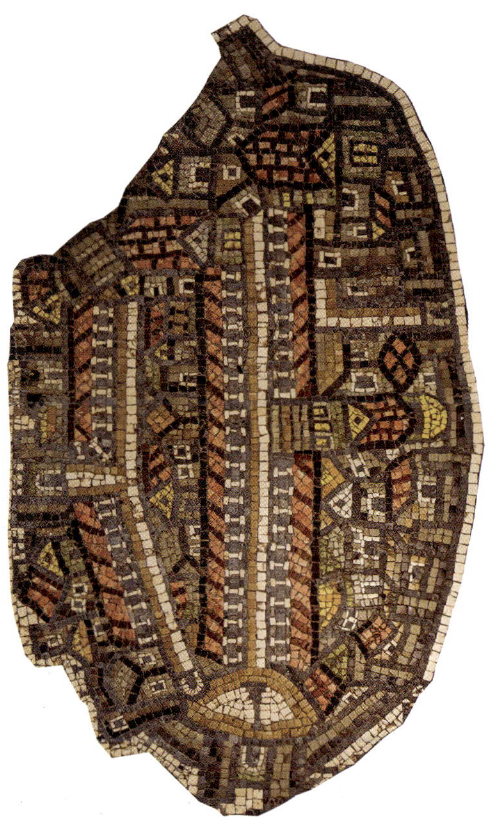

Img. 181: The Madaba map also shows a city plan matching Aelia Capitolina's. A gate leads into an oval plaza with a pillar in the center. From there, the Cardo Maximus (the main north-south oriented street) leads to the church which commemorated Jesus' death and resurrection.

Img. 182: A model of Byzantine Jerusalem, again from the same angle as the reconstructions above, on display at the Church of Saint Peter in Gallicantu.

Img. 183: Aerial view of the Old City, looking down on the front of the Damascus Gate. Built on top of Hadrian's Gate, the Damascus Gate of today leads into Jerusalem's Old City.

Img. 184: The left entrance of Hadrian's triple gate, which led into Aelia Capitolina, is still visible below the level of today's Damascus Gate.

Img. 185: This is the entry gate to Jerash (in Jordan), also built during the reign of Hadrian. This triple gate serves as a visual parallel to Img. 184, as there was a triple gate that looked much like this one before the modern Damascus Gate was constructed.

Img. 186: This is another picture of Jerash which helps to picture what Aelia Capitolina would have looked like in Hadrian's' day.

Img. 187: This model of Aelia Capitolina is looking at the entrance to the city and down the road to the temple of Venus (on the right). Notice the similarity to Jerash, pictured above. One difference between the two cities however, was that the temple in Jerash was dedicated to Artemis instead of Venus.

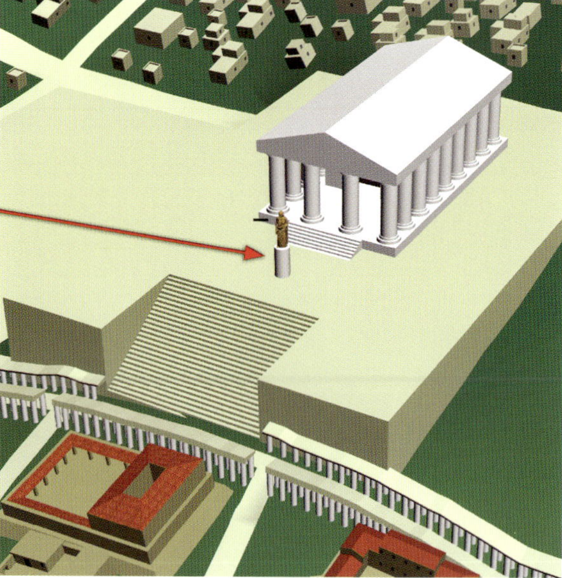

Img. 188: This is the same model (left), zoomed-in on the Jupiter/ Venus temple. The practice of desecrating holy sites and constructing temples over them helped to identify the location of Jesus' tomb. If Jesus had been crucified, buried, and resurrected at Jerash instead of Jerusalem, it would have been logical to look for his tomb underneath the temple of Artemis.

Img. 189: Superimposed over a picture of today's Old City, the horizontal red dashed lines show the orientation of the Cardo Maximus (main street) of Hadrian's day. The vertical red dashed lines mark where the stairs led up to the original entrance of Hadrian's temple and the later church.

Img. 190: These current stairs still follow the original path (note red line) that led to the entrances to Hadrian's temple and the church that was constructed when Hadrian's temple was destroyed.

Img. 191: The southern entrance to the Church of the Holy Sepulchre, pictured here, was constructed in the Medieval Period. Today, this is the main entrance to the building.

the cost for that man's sins with His own life. The second criminal recognized Jesus for who He was—God in the flesh, innocent, yet paying in blood for other's sins. Both criminals died that day: the first in spiritual brokenness, the second with a promise of paradise—forgiven.

After He died, Jesus' body was buried in a nearby tomb in the same garden where He had been crucified. However, on the third day, He was called back into life—resurrected into a new body:

> On the first day of the week, very early in the morning, the women took the spices they had prepared and went to the tomb. They found the stone rolled away from the tomb, but when they entered, they did not find the body of the Lord Jesus. While they were wondering about this, suddenly two men in clothes that gleamed like lightning stood beside them. In their fright the women bowed down with their faces to the ground, but the men said to them, "Why do you look for the living among the dead? He is not here; he has risen!" (Luke 24:1-6)

The Bible promises this same bodily resurrection for all of humanity:

> Multitudes who sleep in the dust of the earth will awake: some to everlasting life, others to shame and everlasting contempt. (Daniel 12:2)
>
> Do not be amazed at this, for a time is coming when all who are in their graves will hear his voice and come out—those who have done what is good will rise to live, and those who have done what is evil will rise to be condemned. (John 5:28-29)

Like Jesus' tomb, at the end of time all the tombs of earth will be emptied. Both criminals who died with Jesus will be called from their graves. They will rise up in a relationship with God—the relationship they chose before their death. The soul of the one who chose Jesus will come from Paradise and rise bodily to everlasting life, while the other who rejected Jesus will rise condemned. In the perfection of the Garden of Eden, man's disobedience opened the door to death. Jesus' perfect obedience in the garden of Golgotha restored the way to life: "For since death came through a man, the resurrection of the dead comes also through a man. For as in Adam all die, so in Christ all will be made alive" (1 Corinthians 15:21-22).

No one has a choice about whether or not to exist for the rest of eternity. We were created for eternity. But like the two criminals, we all must make a choice that will determine how we exist in eternity: believe God and be restored to Eden-like relationship, or mock God and choose eternal separation—forgiveness and restoration freely offered but forever rejected. The choice must be made while we still live. In the garden, Jesus chose death so that we can choose life.

NOTES

1. Josephus and Maier, *Josephus: The Essential Writings*, 264.

2. Tacitus, *Annals of Tacitus*, trans. A. J. Church and W. J. Brodribb (London: Macmillan and Co., 1876), 304.

3. *The Talmud: A Selection*, ed. and trans. Norman Solomon (London: Penguin, 2009), 505.

4. Virgilio C. Corbo, *Il Santo Sepolcro Di Gerusalemme: Aspetti Archeologici Dalle Origini Al Periodo Crociato*, 3 vols., Studium Biblicum Franciscanum Collectio Maior 29 (Jerusalem: Fransciscan Printing Press, 1981).

5. Nahman Avigad, *Discovering Jerusalem* (Jerusalem: Shikmona Publishing Co., 1980), 213–29.

6. Josephus. *The Complete Works*, trans. William Whiston (Nashville: Thomas Nelson, 1998), 844.

7. Shimon Gibson and Joan E. Taylor, *Beneath the Church of the Holy Sepulchre Jerusalem: The Archaeology and Early History of Traditional Golgotha* (London: Committee of the Palestine Exploration Fund, 1994), 61. See also Finegan, *The Archaeology of the New Testament*, 222.

8. Taylor, *Christians and the Holy Places,* 117.

9. For walls covered from Hadrian's temple, see Corbo, The Church of the Holy Sepulchre in Jerusalem, plates 10, 16, 19, 24, 40–44, 61:2a, 62:c, photos 30–31, 34, 44.I, 2, 45.I, 53, 88–90, 97. And for the altar see Florentino Diez Fernandez, *Basilica of the Holy Sepulchre: The Excavations, Archaeological Research*, trans. Freeman-Grenville G.B.P. (The Palestine Exploration Fund, 1984), 34–35, fig. 55.

10. Eusebius, *The Life of the Blessed Emperor Constantine*, 137.

11. Jerome, *St. Jerome: Letters and Select Works*, 120.

12. Eusebius, *The Life of the Blessed Emperor Constantine*, 138.

13. Ibid., 138–39.

14. Shimon Gibson, *The Final Days of Jesus: The Archaeological Evidence* (New York: HarperOne, 2009), 122. See also Athenase Economopolous, *Archaeological Findings in the Church of the Holy Sepulchre in Jerusalem* (Israel Antiquities Authorities Archives, 1971). See also Gibson and Taylor, Beneath the Church, 74.

15. Eusebius, *The Life of the Blessed Emperor Constantine*, 143–44.

16. Ibid., 141.

17. J. W. Crowfoot, *Early Churches in Palestine*, The Schweich Lectures on Biblical Archaeology (London: Published for the British Academy by H. Milford, Oxford University Press, 1941), 10.

18. Eusebius, *Life of Constantine*, quoted in Peters, *Jerusalem: The Holy City*, 133

19. Bordeaux Pilgrim, *Itinerary*, quoted in Peters, *Jerusalem: The Holy City*, 145.

20. Egeria, *Pilgrimage*, quoted in Peters, *Jerusalem: The Holy City*, 140, 148–49.

21. Crowfoot, *Early Churches in Palestine*, 10.

Chapter 9

THE HIGH PLACE

The most commanding view of ancient Jerusalem is from atop the Mount of Olives. Named for the olive groves that have covered it for centuries, the Mount of Olives stands looking down over Mount Moriah. Prophetic expectation has hung over this mountain since Zechariah spoke these words:

> Then the LORD will go out and fight against those nations, as he fights on a day of battle. On that day his feet will stand on the Mount of Olives, east of Jerusalem, and the Mount of Olives will be split in two from east to west, forming a great valley, with half the mountain moving north and half moving south. (Zechariah 14:3-4)

While the Mount of Olives is still intact and awaiting Christ's dramatic return, it has already been the location of several significant scenes in the story of the Messiah.

In the early twentieth century, the ruins of a Crusader-era church marked a spot near to the summit of the Mount of Olives. The question that intrigued everyone at the time was, *What was underneath those ruins?* In 1910 Louis-Hugues

Img. 192: This photo shows the excavations of L. H. Vincent, which began in 1910 on top of the Mount of Olives.

Img. 193: An ancient doorway leading to the excavated Crusader-Period church.

Img. 194: Aerial view of the Mount of Olives. The location of L. H. Vincent's excavation is identified by the red arrow.

Vincent began excavating and soon uncovered the remains of earlier churches that had been built, destroyed, and rebuilt over a long period of time. Seeing these layers, Vincent had no doubt that he was digging a long-venerated site.

THE CHURCH

The oldest of these churches dated to the reign of Constantine, and enough of the foundation trenches from the original building were recovered to enable Vincent to draw a plan of the church's basic structure.[1] Beneath the church's apse was a sacred cave, and like the Nativity cave in Bethlehem, this cave had also been in use in the first century AD.

Having examined the churches at Mamre, Bethlehem, and Jerusalem, this church which Vincent's excavation uncovered is the last of the four Constantinian churches we will study.[2] Details found in biblical and historical texts can enable us to understand why Constantine built this church on the Mount of Olives. We'll begin by looking in the Gospel of Matthew.

In chapter twenty-four, Matthew opens with an account of Jesus leaving the temple area, having just informed His disciples of a coming day when the temple would be destroyed. After He finished teaching, He withdrew to the Mount of Olives. Following Him, the disciples wanted to know more:

> As Jesus was sitting on the Mount of Olives, the disciples came to him privately. "Tell us," they said, "when will this happen, and what will be the sign of your coming and of the end of the age?" (Matthew 24:3)

Sitting on the Mount of Olives, Jesus answered their questions. But he didn't encourage them that He would one day return, plant His feet on the Mount, and fight against Israel's enemies, as they were expecting based on Zechariah's prophecy. Instead, He described a dire future that would unfold: false Christs, wars, famines, and earthquakes, followed by an increase of lawlessness, false prophets, great persecution, and the betrayal of many.

Jesus finished His teaching that day by telling them what He would soon have to undergo:

> When Jesus had finished saying all these things, he said to his disciples, "As you know, the Passover is two days away—and the Son of Man will be handed over to be crucified." (Matthew 26:1-2)

When the disciples left the Mount of Olives with Jesus that day, they did not understand what they had heard; they did not understand what was coming; and they did not know that they would find themselves in that same spot again, listening to Jesus.

When they did return, it was with a resurrected Jesus. He again spoke to them there, giving them His last teaching:

> "But you will receive power when the Holy Spirit comes on you; and you will be my witnesses in Jerusalem, and in all Judea and Samaria, and to the ends of the earth." After he said this, he was taken up before their very eyes, and a cloud hid him from their sight. They were looking intently up into the sky as he was going, when suddenly two men dressed in white stood beside them. "Men of Galilee," they said, "why do you stand here looking into the sky? This same Jesus, who has been taken from you into heaven, will come back in the

Img. 195: This is Eleona Church, looking east toward the church's apse, which is under the raised floor at the top of the steps.

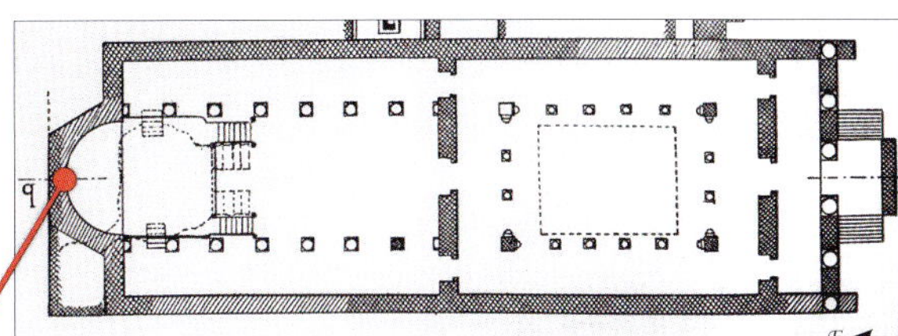

Img. 196: To the right is Vincent's drawing which defines the basic structure of the Constantinian Church which he began excavating in 1910.

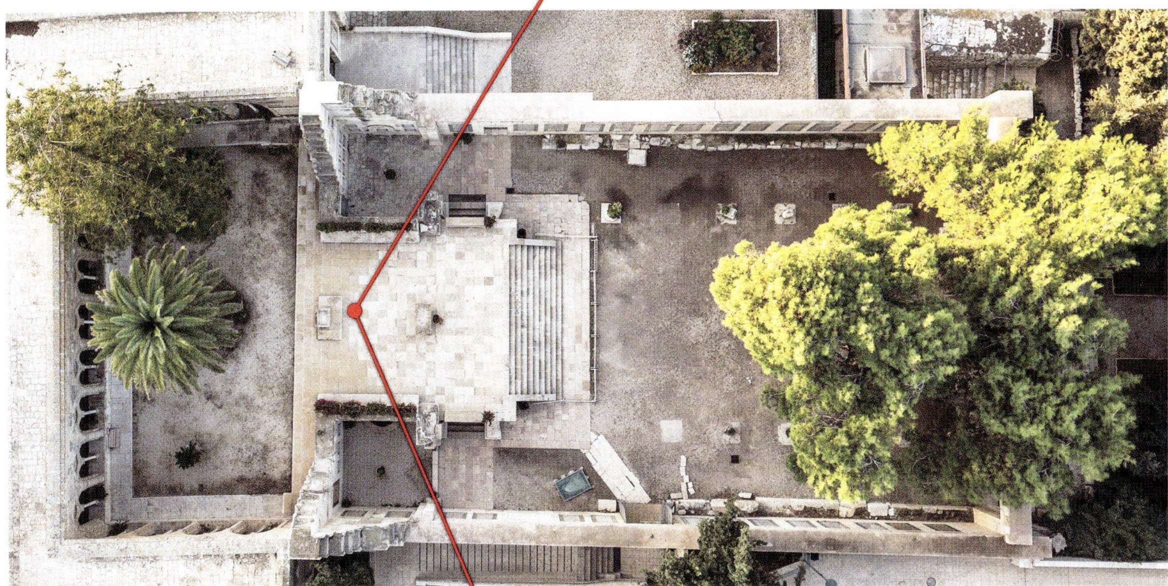

Img. 197: Aerial view of the present-day church grounds with a raised floor covering the apse. Note the red line correlating the location of the apse with Vincent's drawing.

Img. 198: The sacred cave commemorated by the Eleona Church is located beneath the raised floor. The apse from Constantine's church is seen in the half circle formed by the cut stones at the front (east) side of the cave.

> same way you have seen him go into heaven." Then the apostles returned to Jerusalem from the hill called the Mount of Olives. (Acts 1:8-12)

Jesus was gone from earth. The location He departed from was understandably a very important spot to Christians and became holy ground. Early church sources and archaeology help us to validate this location on the Mount of Olives.

Writing around AD 318, some six years before Constantine won the East, Eusebius states:

> According to the common and received account, the feet of our Lord and Saviour, himself the Word of God, truly stood...upon the Mount of Olives at the cave that is shown there. On the ridge of the Mount of Olives he prayed and handed on to his disciples the mysteries of the end, and after this he made his ascension into Heaven, as Luke teaches in the Acts of the Apostles.[3]

The location of this teaching is specified further in Mark's Gospel, which claims, "Jesus was sitting on the Mount of Olives opposite the temple" (Mark 13:3). Eleven years later, around AD 329, Eusebius wrote about a pilgrimage visit to the Mount of Olives by Helena, Constantine's mother.[4] At this time, Helena dedicated the sacred place where another commemorative church was erected:

> She dedicated two sanctuaries to the God whom she worshiped, one at the Cave of the Nativity and the other at the Mount of the Ascension . . . the empress-mother erected a stately edifice on the Mount of Olives as a monument . . . raising a sacred church and sanctuary on the mountain ridge, at the very summit of the hill. Here, in the cave, a true account has it that the Savior of all mankind had initiated His disciples into sacred mysteries.[5]

This "stately edifice" was called *Eleona*, a Greek word meaning "olive grove."[6] Eusebius's account informs us that the Eleona church commemorated the place where Jesus taught His disciples the mysteries of the end of the world and then ascended into heaven.

In about AD 380, the pilgrim Egeria recorded her visit to the church, stating that she went "to the Mount of Olives, to the church on the mountain itself, from which the Lord ascended into heaven after his Passion."[7]

Like the other Constantinian churches, the Eleona church was also destroyed and rebuilt multiple times. Unfortunately, we can no longer see the original structure. Much of what is seen at the site today is from the Crusader Period or later.

Img. 199: The location Vincent excavated matches the descriptions in Mark's Gospel. The Eleona Church (lower left corner in picture) marks the location where Jesus and his disciples sat, looking up at the Temple (marked today by the Dome of the Rock, upper right in picture.) From this sacred spot, Jesus ascended and disappeared into the clouds.

Img. 200: This aerial view shows the Kidron Valley running between the Temple Mount and the Mount of Olives. Gathered with his disciples and looking out over the temple, Jesus taught His disciples about the end of the world and what was to come. The Eleona Church marks the location where He ascended and where He will one day return to fulfill all things

THE INTERPRETATION

The disciples lived out the words Jesus spoke over them as He rose up into heaven from the Mount of Olives. The gospel did indeed spread throughout the world. Because that gospel came to us, now we are also Christ's disciples, and we have the same questions His disciples had so long ago: *When will these things happen? Jesus, when will you return?*

Our answer is the same that He gave to His disciple on the Mount of Olives.

> "But about that day or hour no one knows, not even the angels in heaven, nor the Son, but only the Father. As it was in the days of Noah, so it will be at the coming of the Son of Man. For in the days before the flood, people were eating and drinking, marrying and giving in marriage, up to the day Noah entered the ark; and they knew nothing about what would happen until the flood came and took them all away. That is how it will be at the coming of the Son of Man. Two men will be in the field; one will be taken and the other left. Two women will be grinding with a hand mill; one will be taken and the other left. Therefore keep watch, because you do not know on what day your Lord will come." (Matthew 24:36-42)

Jesus did not give specific dates or times of His return. Instead He gave this strong admonition: *Be awake, alert, and ready, and spread the message that I am the way to life.*

His words were true for the disciples and they are still just as true for us today. Their hope for His return is our hope for His return: "'And this gospel of the kingdom will be preached in the whole world as a testimony to all nations, and then the end will come'" (Matthew 24:14).

Today, it is possible to stand on the Mount of Olives, that same ground where Jesus taught, peer up into the sky, and to try to imagine what it must have felt like to watch Him ascend.

Atop the Mount of Olives, today's Church of the Pater Noster stands right next to the ruins of the 4th-century Byzantine Church of Eleona (facing page). From there, with the Temple clearly in view across the Kidron valley, Jesus warned His disciples about its coming destruction. And, from there, with instructions to wait for the coming of the Holy Spirit, the disciples watched Jesus ascend up to heaven.

Img. 201: An aerial photo showing the Church of the Holy Sepulchre, where Jesus died and rose again; the Dome of the Rock, where the temple stood at the time of Jesus; and Eleona Church, where Jesus ascended and will return. The Dome of the Rock is the lowest in elevation, the Church of the Holy Sepulchre is higher, and the Mount of Olives is the highest of these holy places.

And, while it is a profound experience to ponder what occurred there centuries ago, it is also important to remember the words that the angel spoke to the disciples: "Why do you stand here looking into the sky? This same Jesus, who has been taken . . . into heaven, will come back" (Acts 1:11). He will come back, but not until "this gospel of the kingdom has been preached in the whole world as a testimony" (Matthew 24:14). And, also like the disciples, we are to be His witnesses "to the end of the earth."

The disciples began preaching the gospel to the world, and we continue it. It is possible that we will see what they did not—Christ returning and planting His feet on the Mount of Olives. On that day the Mount of Olives will split between east and west. In the same way, mankind will be split: those who have believed Christ will be part of the Kingdom of God, and those who have rejected Christ will not. Come quickly, Lord Jesus. But until that day, let us be awake, alert, and ready, urgently spreading the news—the Kingdom of God is at hand.

NOTES

1. Finegan, *The Archaeology of the New Testament*, 167-68.

2. L. H. Vincent, "L'église De L'éléona," Revue Biblique (1892–1940) 7, no. 4 (1910): 573–74. L. H. Vincent was present at the excavations of the Eleona church and wrote a report about it.

3. Eusebius, *The Proof of the Gospel,* 2:30.

4. John Wilkenson, "Christian Worship in the Byzantine Period," in *Ancient Churches Revealed* , ed. Yoram Tsafrir (Jerusalem: Israel Exploration Society, 1993) 23.

5. Eusebius, *Life of Constantine*, quoted in F. E. Peters, *Jerusalem: The Holy City*, 137.

6. Finegan, *The Archaeology of the New Testament*, 165.

7. Egeria, *Pilgrimage*, quoted in F. E. Peters, *Jerusalem: The Holy City*, 140.

Jerusalem's Western Hill is hemmed in by the valley of Ben Hinnom on its western and southern borders. On top of this hill, another critical biblical event took place.

Chapter 10
THE UPPER ROOM

In 1859, Jerusalem's Municipal Engineer, Ermete Pierotti, made a note while investigating the top of Jerusalem's Western Hill. He wrote,

> I discovered, by means of an examination I made from the exterior [of the building] the walls of an ancient Jewish building, mixed, in the parts above the floor, with later construction, which had been inserted during repairs.[1]

Years later, the structure Pierotti had noticed was struck by a mortar shell in the 1948 Arab–Israeli War. Subsequently, an Israeli archaeologist, Jacob Pinkerfeld, conducted a salvage excavation to prepare the damaged building for repair.[2] His excavation revealed that the largest and oldest stones used in this building's foundations dated to the Roman Period. On the north side, these Roman-Period stones formed a niche at the front of the ancient building. Pinkerfeld recognized this

Img. 202: This is L. H. Vincent's drawing from the early 1900s of what Pierotti called "an old Jewish Building."

Img. 203: A picture of the same building as the drawing to the left. The mixture of masonry styles, which Pierotti observed in 1859, can still be seen today with the larger and oldest stones on the bottom.

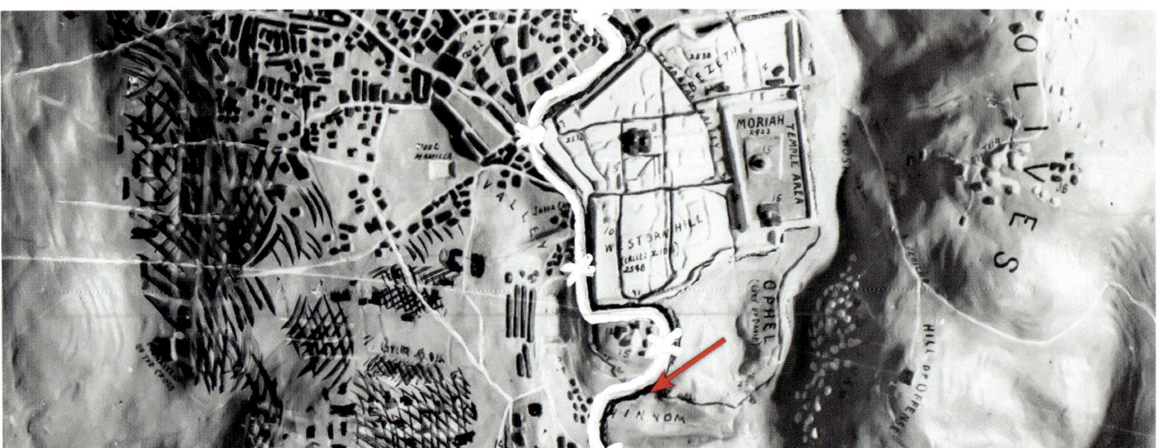

Img. 204: The white line in this image marks the 1948 border between Jordan and Israel. The red arrow points out the approximate position of the building excavated by the Jewish archaeologist Jacob Pinkerfeld, on the south side of Jerusalem's Old City, just inside the Israeli side of the border.

Img. 205: The building excavated by Pinkerfeld is currently used as a synagogue, just as he interpreted that it was used for when it was constructed over 1,900 years ago. This picture shows three young Jewish men worshiping in front of the original synagogue's Torah Ark, used to house the Hebrew scriptures, dating all the way back to the first century AD.

Img. 206: This is a view of the synagogue and its dome in proximity to Dormition Abbey.

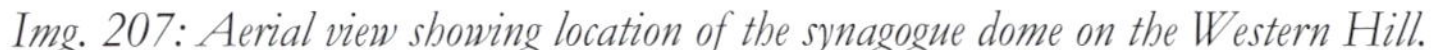

Img. 207: Aerial view showing location of the synagogue dome on the Western Hill.

Img. 208: A close-up of the synagogue and dome.

Img. 209: From the Ben Hinnom Valley (below), looking uphill and to the north, the synagogue's dome is visible.

to be the type of niche used in ancient Jewish synagogues and interpreted the niche, often called a Torah Ark, as the place within the synagogue where the sacred scrolls of the Hebrew Bible (Old Testament) were kept for public reading.[3]

In his summary of Pinkerfeld's excavation, archaeologist J. W. Hirshberg wrote the following:

> Pinkerfeld reached the conclusion that the . . . chamber [niche] represents a synagogue erected in the first centuries after the destruction of the Second Temple. He based this on the following factors: The construction is Roman; the niche faces the Temple site, like the niches found in the synagogues at Eshtemoa and Nave (used as Holy Arks for keeping Torah scrolls).[4]

Pinkerfeld's excavations dug down through different floor levels showing the building's use over a long period of time. Writing about the earliest floor level he discovered, Pinkerfeld recorded,

> Seventy cm below the present floor level another floor of plaster was found . . . It is certain that this floor belonged to the original building, i.e., to the period when the northern wall and its apse [niche] were built.[5]

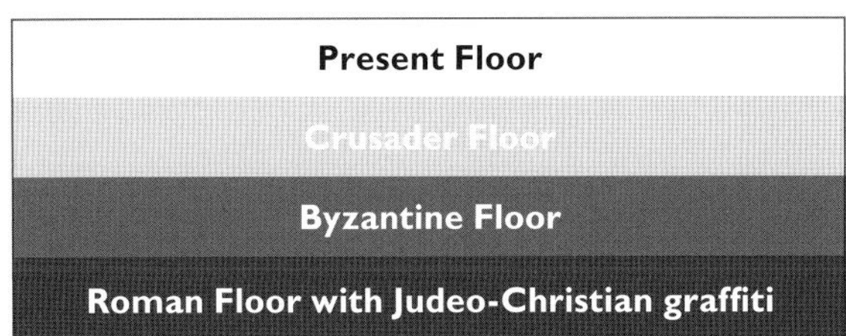

Img. 210: The different floor levels Pinkerfeld excavated and recorded.

Pinkerfeld also discovered pieces of plaster containing graffiti (wall writings/markings) that had fallen from the walls of the original synagogue building. Tragically, before he was able to publish the graffiti, Pinkerfeld was killed. On September 23, 1956, while touring an archaeological site just north of Jerusalem, Pinkerfeld and three other archaeologists were shot down by a sniper. Eventually, however, the graffiti found on the plaster pieces was published. Two of the Greek inscriptions were translated as, "Conquer, O Saviour, Mercy" and "Oh, Jesus, that I may live."[6]

Based on this new evidence, the building which Pinkerfeld had understood to be a traditional Jewish synagogue was reinterpreted by others as being a Judeo-Christian synagogue.[7] Archaeologist Bellarmino Bagatti explained, "Pinkerfeld, followed by Avi-Yonah, believes that the synagogue was Jewish, unaware of the existence of Judeo-Christian synagogues."[8]

The existence of synagogues showing a combination of Jewish and Christian influence is known through several independent historical sources. In fact, different early sources identified the existence of a Judeo-Christian synagogue on the Western Hill.

Eusebius informs us of a church that is even older than those Constantine had built in Jerusalem. "Tradition has it that up to the time of Hadrian's siege there was a very large church of Christ in Jerusalem which was constructed by Jews."[9]

Why would Eusebius call a building built by Jews a church? Because the earliest followers of Jesus were Jewish, and the Greek-speaking, Jewish Christ followers would have continued calling their houses of worship synagogues, which is a Greek word simply meaning "assembly."[10] Later Christian worship buildings began to be called churches, which is why by AD 318, Eusebius called the synagogue on the Western Hill a "church . . . constructed by Jews."

Img. 211: This is he basic plan of the original first century AD synagogue building.

Img. 212: Surprisingly, the Torah Ark niche was found not to point in the direction of the Jewish temple where the Dome of the Rock currently stands (longest dashed arrow). Instead, the niche aimed directly toward the place of resurrection, which is marked today by the Church of the Holy Sepulchre (shorter dashed arrow).

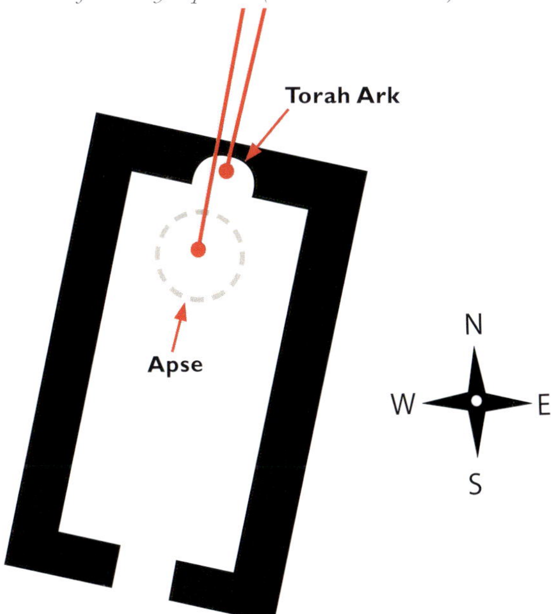

Img. 213: This is a plan of the first century AD synagogue-church, showing its correlation to the present-day building and its orientation toward the Church of the Holy Sepulchre.

Regardless, the pilgrim from Bordeaux still refers to this building as a synagogue when he sees it on his visit to Jerusalem in AD 333: "Of the seven synagogues which once stood there [on the Western Hill], only one remains; the others are ploughed under and gone to seed, as Isaiah [1:8] has said." [11]

What is clear is that the "church … constructed by Jews" which Eusebius recorded in AD 318, the remaining synagogue which the Bordeaux pilgrim described in AD 333, the "ancient Jewish building" Pierotti identified in 1859, and the synagogue which Pinkerfeld later excavated are all the same building.

In addition, this building had a unique feature which helps to further confirm its being correctly understood as Judeo-Christian. The niche that held the Torah scrolls did not point toward the temple, as Pinkerfeld assumed and as would be normal for a typical Jewish synagogue. Instead, it was found to point more toward the north, directly at what is today the Church of the Holy Sepulchre.

Scholar Bargil Pixner published his analysis about the niche:

> Was this directional orientation intentional? I believe it was. Would it not be logical that, after the Temple had been destroyed, Judeo-Christians, instead of orienting their synagogues toward the destroyed Temple as was the case with traditional Jews, would orient their synagogues toward the new center of their redemption, the site of Jesus' burial and resurrection?[12]

We must keep in mind that when this Judeo-Christian synagogue was built, its Torah niche pointed toward the garden where Golgotha and the empty tomb were located. At the time of the building's construction, just after AD 70, Golgotha and the tomb of Jesus would have still remained relatively undisturbed. It would be about eighty years before Hadrian would desecrate the site with his temple and around two hundred fifty years before Constantine would build the Martyrium and Anastasis.

Img. 214: See the synagogue church building in the foreground (bottom-most red arrow) and the Church of the Holy Sepulchre in the background (top-most red arrow).

So the orientation of the Torah niche alerts us that this building was built by Christ-following Jews. But why was it built? What does this synagogue-church commemorate? To find an answer, we must once again turn to the pages of the New Testament.

> Then came the first day of Unleavened Bread on which the Passover lamb had to be sacrificed. And Jesus sent Peter and John, saying, "Go and prepare the Passover for us, so that we may eat it." They said to Him, "Where do You want us to prepare it?" And He said to them, "When you have entered the city, a man will meet you carrying a pitcher of water; follow him into the house that he enters. And you shall say to the owner of the house, 'The Teacher says to you, Where is the guest room in which I may eat the Passover with My disciples?' And he will show you a large, furnished upper room; prepare it there." And they left and found everything just as He had told them; and they prepared the Passover. ... And when He had taken some bread and given thanks, He broke it and gave it to them, saying, "This is My body which is given for you; do this in remembrance of Me." And in the same way He took the cup after they had eaten, saying, "This cup which is poured out for you is the new covenant in My blood." (Luke 22:7-13, 19-20 NASB)

This event, known as the Last Supper, took place in "a large ... upper room" (v. 12) the day before Jesus was crucified.

In the first chapter of Acts, we see another reference to Jesus' followers all gathered together after His ascension. They united in a house that had a room large enough for 120 people (Acts 1:15) to sit and wait to receive what Jesus had promised:

> When the day of Pentecost came, they were all together in one place. Suddenly a sound like the blowing of a violent wind came from heaven and filled the whole house where they were sitting. They saw

> what seemed to be tongues of fire that separated and came to rest on each of them. All of them were filled with the Holy Spirit and began to speak in other tongues as the Spirit enabled them. (Acts 2:1-4)

This house with its large upper room would have been destroyed along with the rest of Jerusalem in AD 70. However, the archaeological evidence indicates that not long afterward, Jewish followers of Jesus returned to Jerusalem and built a place of assembly over the ruins of the house where the Last Supper and Pentecost had taken place. They included in their construction of the synagogue a Torah niche pointing directly at Golgotha and the tomb of resurrection. This venerated building still stood on top of the Western Hill, which the Byzantines by this time called Mount Zion, when an early bishop named Epiphanius (AD 315–403) wrote about it:

> When the Roman emperor Hadrian visited Jerusalem in AD 130/131, there was standing on Mt. Zion [Western Hill] "a small church of God. It marked the site of the Hypero-on (Upper Room) to which the disciples returned from the Mount of Olives after the Lord had been taken up." [13]

Unsurprisingly then, the veneration of this "small church of God" continued for centuries. Around AD 382, an octagonal-shaped Byzantine church

Img. 215: After the house and upper room were destroyed in AD 70, the early Jewish followers of Jesus built a synagogue over its ruins (black).

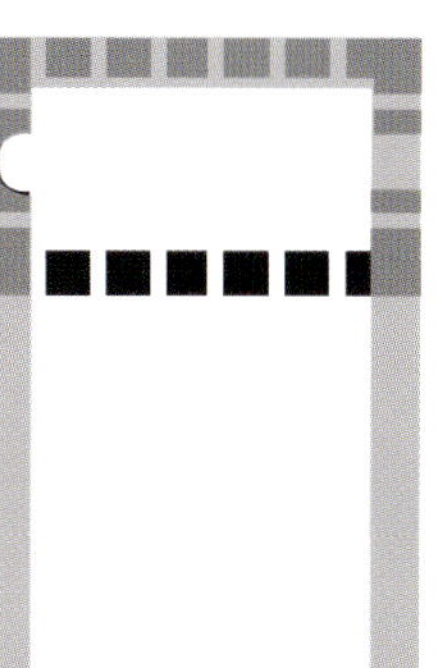

Img. 216: Later, the original synagogue building was expanded (grey). This larger building was called the Church of the Apostles.

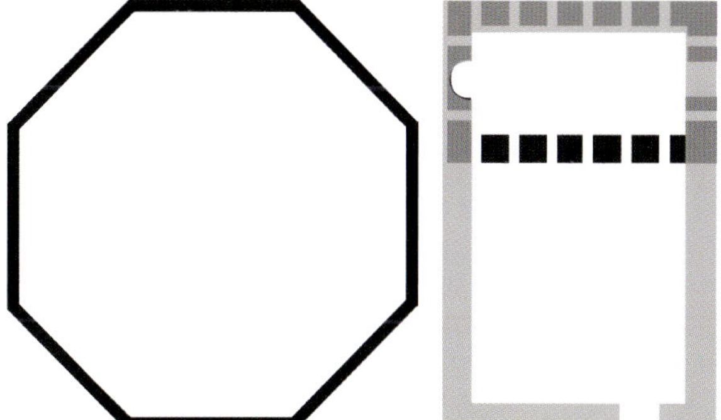

Img. 217: In the fourth century AD, an octagonal-shaped Byzantine church was built next to, rather than on top of, the Church of the Apostles.

Img. 218: This mosaic in the Church of Santa Pudenziana in Rome, shows the Byzantine Church and the Church of the Apostles just to the right of Jesus, who is seated on His throne.

Img. 219: This close-up from the picture above clearly shows the octagonal Byzantine church on the left and the Judeo-Christian synagogue on the right.

was built next to, rather than on top of, the original Judeo-Christian synagogue. This indicates the possibility that both buildings were being used during this time, one by Jewish and the other by Gentile worshipers of Jesus Christ. In this time the old Judeo-Christian structure was called the Church of the Apostles.

The mosaic, which we discussed in chapter 8, preserved in the church in Rome and dating to about AD 400, shows both buildings. Seen behind and to the right of the enthroned Jesus is the octagonal Byzantine church. Next to it and further to the right is a more ancient-looking building. Amazingly, this mosaic-captured image is more than 1,600 years old and shows the actual synagogue building used by the early Jewish followers of Jesus. This is the synagogue church on the Western Hill of Jerusalem where the Last Supper and Pentecost took place, reported by early Christians, observed by Pierotti in 1859, and excavated by Pinkerfeld in the early 1950s.

Around AD 415, the octagonal church was replaced by a much larger Byzantine church called the Hagia Sion Basilica.[14] The Church of the Apostles, which included the original Judeo-Christian synagogue, remained next to it.

Img. 220: This is a plan of the larger Byzantine church, which was called the Hagia Sion, next to the Church of the Apostles.

Img. 221: This is a plan of the Crusader Church that still stands today. The lower floor, which was the old Judeo-Christian synagogue, currently functions as a synagogue, while the upper floor is a church.

Img. 222: Above is the Madaba map with a section of the mosaic blown up. The close-up clearly shows the Hagia Sion Church on the left side and the synagogue church immediately next to it on the right side.

Img. 223: Jewish worshipers reading the Torah and praying within the remains of the old Judeo-Christian synagogue. Notice the large stones in the lower courses of masonry that date all the way back to the first century AD, when the ruins of the house with the upper room were rebuilt into a synagogue by the early followers of Jesus.

These two churches are depicted on the oldest preserved map of the Holy Land, also discussed in chapter 8. In Jordan, the sixth-century Madaba Map mosaic depicts two buildings at the southern end of the Cardo Maximus (Main Street). The larger building on the left is the Hagia Sion Church, and next to it is the smaller synagogue church.

These churches were destroyed in the Persian invasion of Jerusalem in AD 614 and soon rebuilt, only to be destroyed again by Muslim invaders in AD 1009. The Crusaders rebuilt the church around AD 1110, but it was again destroyed and rebuilt by the Crusaders once more in 1219. This Crusader church continued to incorporate the foundational remains of the original Judeo-Christian synagogue. In the later years, Muslims converted the old Judeo-Christian synagogue church into a mosque; however, after 1948 and until today, this sacred space functions as a Jewish synagogue.

THE INTERPRETATION

To understand the significance of what happened in that room on top of the Western Hill, we must have some understanding about people's Messianic expectations at the time of Christ. The prophet Samuel had written,

> "The Lord declares to you that the Lord himself will establish a house for you: When your days are over and you rest with your ancestors, I will raise up your offspring to succeed you, your own flesh and blood, and I will establish his kingdom. He is the one who will build a house [temple] for my Name, and I will establish the throne of his kingdom forever." (2 Samuel 7:11-13)

While Solomon was David's offspring, and while he did build a glorious temple, Solomon was not the one God was speaking of who would "build a house for my Name" and a "kingdom forever."

God also spoke of the coming temple builder through the prophet Zechariah:

> Tell him this is what the Lord Almighty says: "Here is the man whose name is the Branch, and he will branch out from his place and build the temple of the Lord. It is he who will build the temple of the Lord." . . . Those who are far away will come and help to build the temple of the Lord, and you will know that the Lord Almighty has sent me to you. (Zechariah 6:12-13, 15 NASB)

Because of these and other similar prophecies, people's anticipation was that the coming Messiah would build a temple for the Lord. Jesus perfectly fulfilled this Messianic requirement, but not in the way that anyone anticipated.

For the Jews to truly recognize Jesus as their Messiah, He would have to build a temple more glorious than Solomon's. But how could He do that? There was already a standing temple, built by Zerubbabel in 516 BC, which Herod the Great had spent years enlarging and enhancing to restore to its former Solomonic glory. Would that temple have to be destroyed and rebuilt? Yes, a temple would have to be destroyed then rebuilt, but not the one that the people were thinking of:

> "Destroy this temple, and I will raise it again in three days." They replied, "It has taken forty-six years to build this temple, and you are going to raise it in three days?" But the temple he had spoken of was his body. (John 2:19-21)

No one understood Him. Everyone's expectations, including His disciples', were focused on the physical temple, yet Jesus knew that He would have to be destroyed before He could be raised.

In preparation for what would soon come, Jesus gathered His disciples together in the upper room on the Western Hill. There He broke bread and drank wine with them and urged them to always remember what He was going to undergo. "For as often as you eat this bread and drink the cup, you proclaim the Lord's death until he comes" (1 Corinthians 11:26). The next day He would lay Himself down as the chief cornerstone of the glorious temple He would build.

The disciples experienced all that Jesus promised would come to pass. They watched Him being crucified. They saw and touched His resurrected body. They witnessed His glorious ascent into heaven. And, as He had instructed them to, they remembered. The early Jewish followers of Jesus gathered together in that upper room to break bread and drink wine in remembrance of all Christ had done for them.

Jesus had also instructed His followers to wait there in that room, promising that He would pour out His Spirit on them. They did wait, and when the day came, the room was filled with tongues of fire as the Spirit of God descended and filled His people. However, the upper room could not contain what was happening, and the power of the Spirit flowed out into Jerusalem.

> Now there were staying in Jerusalem God-fearing Jews from every nation under heaven. When they heard the sound, a crowd came together in bewilderment, because each one heard their own language being spoken. Utterly amazed, they asked: "Aren't all these who are speaking Galileans? Then how is it that each of us hears them in our native language? Parthians, Medes and Elamites; residents of Mesopotamia, Judea and Cappadocia, Pontus and Asia, Phrygia and Pamphylia, Egypt and the parts of Libya near Cyrene; visitors from Rome (both Jews and converts to Judaism); Cretans and Arabs—we hear them declaring the wonders of God in our own tongues!" Amazed and perplexed, they asked one another, "What does this mean?" Then Peter stood up with the Eleven, raised his voice and addressed the crowd: "Fellow Jews and all of you who live in Jerusalem, let me explain this to you; listen carefully to what I say." (Acts 2:5-12, 14)

The words of Zechariah were being fulfilled: "Those who are far away will come and help to build the temple of the LORD" (6:15). The cornerstone of a new temple had been set in place with Christ's death and resurrection. The apostles and prophets were the foundation that God laid. And now this new and living temple was being raised up with people "from every nation under heaven." It would continue to grow as the message of the gospel went out. That day Peter declared,

> "Fellow Israelites, listen to this: Jesus of Nazareth was a man accredited by God to you by miracles, wonders and signs, which God did among you through him, as you yourselves know. This man was handed over to you by God's deliberate plan and foreknowledge; and you, with the help of wicked men, put him to death by nailing him to the cross. But God raised him from the dead, freeing him from the agony of death, because it was impossible for death to keep its hold on him." When the people heard this, they were cut to the heart and said to Peter and the other apostles, "Brothers, what shall we do?" Peter replied, "Repent and be baptized, every one of you, in the name of Jesus Christ for the forgiveness of your sins. And you will receive the gift of the Holy Spirit. The promise is for you and your children and for all who are far off—for all whom the Lord our God will call." With many other words he warned them; and he pleaded with them, "Save yourselves from this corrupt generation." Those who accepted his message were baptized, and about three thousand were added to their number that day. (Acts 2:22-24, 37-41)

After that day, the upper room could not hold the ever-growing number of Christ followers. But its purpose had been fulfilled: it marked the special place where Jesus had shared His last meal with the disciples. It was revered as the place from which Christ's Spirit had flowed into this world, commemorating the birth of the church.

In time, those Jewish believers built a synagogue where the room had stood, a Christ-worshiping synagogue with a Torah niche aimed toward the place where their Messiah had died and risen. Soon, a church was built next to that synagogue, referred to as the Mother of all Churches because it was the first church. More churches were built over that first church, all marking and honoring that first gathering place—the Upper Room.

Today, it is possible to travel to Jerusalem from various countries and stand in the place that marks the upper room. While we cannot sit at the table with Jesus or experience tongues of fire roaring over our heads, we can know that we are still connected to the events that happened there, because we are connected to Christ. The Apostle Peter taught,

> As you come to him, the living Stone—rejected by humans but chosen by God and precious to him—you also, like living stones, are being built into a spiritual house to be a holy priesthood, offering spiritual sacrifices acceptable to God through Jesus Christ. (1 Peter 2:4-5)

This living temple, birthed in Jerusalem almost two thousand years ago, now fills the earth—and we are part of it. May our lives be like that upper room: full of remembrance of Christ's sacrifice and filled with His Spirit.

NOTES

1. J. W. Hirschberg, "The Remains of an Ancient Synagogue on Mount Zion," in *Jerusalem Revealed: Archaeology in the Holy City 1968–1974*, ed. Yigael Yadin (Jerusalem: The Israel Exploration Society, Mercaz Press, 1976), 117.

2. Bargil Pixner, "Church of the Apostles Found on Mount Zion," *Biblical Archaeology Review XVI*, no. 3, May/June (1990), 23.

3. Ibid.

4. Hirschberg, "The Remains of an Ancient Synagogue," 116.

5. Pixner, "Church of the Apostles Found on Mount Zion," 23.

6. Bagatti, *The Church from the Circumcision,* 121.

7. Ibid.

8. Ibid.

9. Eusebius, *The Proof of the Gospel,* 1:143.

10. Pixner, "Church of the Apostles Found on Mount Zion," 24.

11. Hirschberg, "The Remains of an Ancient Synagogue," 116.

12. Pixner "Church of the Apostles Found on Mount Zion," 24.

13. Baldi, *Enchiridion*, quoted in Pixner "Church of the Apostles Found on Mount Zion," 26.

14. Pixner, "Church of the Apostles Found on Mount Zion," 25.

CONCLUSION

Standing at Bethel, Jacob proclaimed, "How awesome is this place!" (Genesis 28:17). His amazement wasn't due to the beauty or grandeur of the location. He was struck with awe at his encounter with the one who had come down the stairway of heaven to speak to him there. Like Jacob, we can stand and marvel about Jesus as we study and visit the "awesome places" where He met with the saints of old, bringing heaven to earth, accomplishing His task of redemption.

Just as historical events in scripture are not isolated, but instead are intricately connected, so too are the places where they happened. In a tent at Mamre, the LORD's promise to an old, barren woman was ultimately fulfilled almost two thousand years later through a young virgin living in a house in Nazareth.

Long before Jesus' birth, the LORD had directed Abraham to the mountain of Moriah, where He instructed Abraham to sacrifice "your son, your only son, whom you love—Isaac" (Genesis 22:2). Abraham obeyed, and in his willingness to lay Isaac on an altar, we see the foreshadowing of the day at Golgotha where the LORD was willing to sacrifice the life of His only Son because He "so loved the world" (John 3:16).

Unlike Isaac, there could be no substitute for Jesus' life. He was crucified. And with His final breath, the Son of God cried out, "Father, forgive them" (Luke 23:34). At that moment the "gate of heaven" which had descended to Jacob at Bethel again ripped down from heaven to earth through the temple curtain. Split from top to bottom, the veil which had separated most holy Yahweh from sinful people was forevermore torn apart, destroyed. That day, Yahweh's long-given promise was fulfilled—all peoples on earth were blessed with access to God through Jacob's offspring.

Before His death, "Jesus the Messiah, the son of David, the son of Abraham" (Matthew 1:1) had promised that "a time is coming when all who are in their graves will hear his voice and come out" (John 5:28-29). Jesus knew that He would die and be laid in a tomb. But He also knew the psalmist had prophesied that He would not be abandoned to the grave or suffer decay. Three days later, His Father's voice called Him out of that grave. And the day is coming when He will descend on the Mount of Olives and call out to the bones of Abraham and Jacob buried at Machpelah and the bones of David buried in the City of David on the Western Hill to rise, leave their tombs, and follow Him in resurrected life.

Peter also knew the psalmist's words, and after being filled with the Holy Spirit in the upper room, he preached those words to a crowd of curious Jews who had gathered on the Western Hill:

> "Fellow Israelites, I can tell you confidently that the patriarch David died and was buried, and his tomb is here to this day. But he was a prophet and knew that God had promised him on oath that he would place one of his descendants on his throne. Seeing what was to come, he spoke of the resurrection of the Messiah, that he was not abandoned to the realm of the dead, nor did his body see decay. God has raised this Jesus to life, and we are all witnesses of it." Those who accepted his message were baptized, and about three thousand were added to their number that day. (Acts 2:29-31, 41)

Knowing the truth of Peter's words that day was not an issue. Everyone in that crowd knew David's tomb well and knew that his bones were in it. And, by that time, everyone in Jerusalem also knew that Jesus' tomb was empty. But that was the day when many finally accepted the reason for His missing body—He was their Messiah, raised up just as David had written.

From an archaeological standpoint, Jesus was like his forefather, Abraham. Just as nomads living in tents don't leave much behind, neither do travelers staying in other people's houses. Jesus once said, "Foxes have dens and birds have nests, but the Son of Man has no place to lay his head" (Luke 9:58).

As a king, Jesus could have erected magnificent places to exalt Himself as Herod the Great tried to do with his restoration of the temple and the monumental commemorations of Mamre and Machpelah. Earthly buildings and glory were not His plan, however. When Pontius Pilate asked Jesus if He was the King of the Jews, Jesus responded, "My kingdom is not of this world" (John 18:36).

For His true kingdom, Jesus did build something magnificent. Unlike the massive stones which Herod had quarried, cut, and stacked, Jesus built with "living stones" (1 Peter 2:5). And, while Herod's temple has been destroyed, Jesus' temple will last forever:

> Consequently, you are no longer foreigners and strangers, but fellow citizens with God's people and also members of his household, built on the foundation of the apostles and prophets, with Christ Jesus himself as the chief cornerstone. In him the whole building is joined together and rises to become a holy temple in the Lord. And in him you too are being built together to become a dwelling in which God lives by his Spirit. (Ephesians 2:19-22)

Many in His day did not recognize Christ as their Messiah and Savior. Today our world is still greatly blinded to recognizing Jesus and believing in the salvation He offers. But for any who wonder about Him, who are drawn to seek and ask questions, we are called to be His witnesses. We are instructed to be prepared to offer the reason for our hope, to share the evidence for His life, death, and resurrection.

Jesus did that for Thomas, who needed to be sure. When Jesus extended His hands to be examined, Thomas touched the nail holes and declared, "My Lord and my God!" (John 20:28).

Today we can no longer physically touch Jesus, but we do still have the places that He touched, the places where the promises of His coming were made and fulfilled. For some, examining the evidence found in those places will play a role in their coming to believe.

Jesus' kingdom is not yet full. But as we share our hope in Him, it continues to grow. When His building is complete, Jerusalem's final archaeological layer will descend to earth, never to be destroyed again:

> I saw the Holy City, the new Jerusalem, coming down out of heaven from God…
> I did not see a temple in the city, because the Lord God Almighty and the Lamb are its temple. (Revelation 21:2, 22)

JERUSALEM PANORAMA

THE MOUNTAIN OF GOD (MORIAH)
CENTRAL VALLEY
CITY OF DAVID
DAVID'S PALACE
TOMB OF DAVID
KIDRON VALLEY
THE MOUNT OF OLIVES
THE HIGH PLACE
(ELEONA CHURCH)

BIBLIOGRAPHY

Avigad, Nahman. *Discovering Jerusalem.* Jerusalem: Shikmona Publishing Co., 1980.

Bagatti, Bellarmino. *Gli Antichi Edifici Sacri Di Betlemme in Seguito Agli Scavi E Restauri Praticati Dalla Custodia Di Terra Santa (1948-51) PSBF 9.* Jerusalem: Franciscan Printing Press, 1952.

Bagatti, Bellarmino. *Excavations in Nazareth Volume 1: From Beginning Till the Xii Century.* Translated by Eugene Hoade. Jerusalem: Franciscan Printing Press, 1969.

Bagatti, Bellarmino. *The Church from the Circumcision: History and Archaeology of the Judeo-Christians* Studium Biblicum Fransciscanum, Smaller Series. 1984, Reprint. Jerusalem: Franciscan Printing Press, 1971.

Bagatti, Bellarmino and Eugene Hoade. *The Church of the Gentiles in Palestine: History and Archaeology.* Jerusalem: Franciscan Printing Press, 1971.

Cahill, Jane M. and David Tarler. "Excavations Directed by Yigal Shiloh at the City of David, 1978-1985." In *Ancient Jerusalem Revealed*, edited by Hillel Geva, 34-45. Jerusalem: Israel Exploration Society, 2000.

Chadwick, Jeffrey R. "The Archaeology of Biblical Hebron in the Bronze and Iron Ages: An Examination of the Discoveries of the American Expedition to Hebron." PhD diss., University of Utah, 1992.

Corbo, Virgilio C. *Il Santo Sepolcro Di Gerusalemme: Aspetti Archeologici Dalle Origini Al Periodo Crociato.* 3 vols. Studium Biblicum Franciscanum Collectio Maior 29. Jerusalem: Fransciscan Printing Press, 1981.

Crowfoot, J. W. *Early Churches in Palestine.* The Schweich Lectures on Biblical Archaeology. London: Published for the British Academy by H. Milford, Oxford University Press, 1941.

Diez Fernandez, Florentino. *Basilica ofthe Holy Sepulchre: The Excavations, Archaeological Research.* Translated by Freeman-Grenville G.B.P.: The Palestine Exploration Fund, 1984.

Economopolous, Athenase. *Archaeological Findings in the Church ofthe Holy Sepulchre in Jerusalem.* Israel Antiquities Authorities Archives, 1971.

Eusebius. *The Life ofthe Blessed Emperor Constantine.* London: S. Bagster and Sons, 1845.

Eusebius. *The Proofofthe Gospel: Being the Demonstratio Evangelica ofEusebius ofCaesarea* Edited by W. J. Sparrow-Simpson and W. K. L. Clarke. Translated by William John Ferrar. 2 vols. Translations of Christian Literature: Series I: Greek Texts. London; New York: Society for Promoting Christian Knowledge; The Macmillan Company, 1920.

Eusebius, G. S. P. Freeman-Grenville, Rupert L. Chapman, and Joan E. Taylor. *The Onomasticon by Eusebius of Caesarea: Palestine in the Fourth Century A.D.* Jerusalem: Carta, 2003.

Finegan, Jack. *The Archaeology of the New Testament: The Life of Jesus and the Beginning of the Early Church.* Rev. ed. Princeton, NJ: Princeton University Press, 1992.

Finkelstein, Israel and Neil Asher Silberman. *The Bible Unearthed.* New York: Touchstone, 2002.

Garstang, John. *The Foundations of Bible History: Joshua, Judges*. London: Constable & Co. Ltd., 1971.

Geva, Hillel. "Twenty-Five Years of Excavations in Jerusalem, 1967-1992." In *Ancient Jerusalem Revealed*, edited by Hillel Geva, 1-28. Jerusalem: Israel Exploration Society, 2000.

Gibson, Shimon. *The Final Days of Jesus: The Archaeological Evidence*. New York: HarperOne, 2009.

Gibson, Shimon and Joan E. Taylor. *Beneath the Church of the Holy Sepulchre Jerusalem: The Archaeology and Early History of Traditional Golgotha*. London: Committee of the Palestine Exploration Fund, 1994.

Gutman, S. and A. Berman. "Chronique Archéologique." *Revue Biblique* 77 (1970): 583-85.

Hammond, Philip C. "An American Expedition to Hebron" Project Prospectus. Brandeis University, 1964.

Harvey, William. *Structural Survey of the Church of the Nativity, Bethlehem*. London: Oxford University Press, H. Milford, 1935.

Hirschberg, J. W. "The Remains of an Ancient Synagogue on Mount Zion." In *Jerusalem Revealed: Archaeology in the Holy City 1968-1974*, edited by Yigael Yadin, 116-17. Jerusalem: The Israel Exploration Society, Mercaz Press, 1976.

Jerome. *St. Jerome: Letters and Select Works*. Edited by Philip Schaff and Henry Wallace. Translated by W. H. Fremantle, G. Lewis, and W. G. Martley. A Select Library of the Nicene and Post-Nicene Fathers of the Christian Church, Second Series, Vol. 6. New York: Christian Literature Company, 1893.

Josephus, Flavius. "The Wars of the Jews." In *The Complete Works*. translated by William Whiston, 651-925. Nashville: Thomas Nelson, 1998.

Josephus, Flavius and Paul L. Maier. *Josephus: The Essential Writings*. Translated and edited by Paul L. Maier. Grand Rapids, MI: Kregel Publications, 1988.

Kansha, H. "A Byzantine Church at Beitin, Palestine". Paper presented, the Archi-Cultural Interactions Through the Silk Road, 4th International Conference, Nishinomiya, Japan, July 16-18, 2016.

Kelso, James L. *The Excavation of Bethel (1934-1960)*. Cambridge: American Schools of Oriental Research, 1968.

Kenyon, Kathleen M. *Digging up Jerusalem*. London: Ernest Benn Limited, 1974.

Kramer, Joel P. *The Bible vs. Joseph Smith*. DVD. www.sourceflix.com, 2010.

Mader, Andreas Evaristus. *Mambre: Die Ergebnisse Der Ausgrabungen Im Heiligen Bezirk Râmet El-Halîl in Südpalästina 1926-1928*. Freiburg im Breisgau: Erich Wewel Verlag, 1957.

Magen, Yitzhak. "Mamre. A Cultic Site from the Reign of Herod." In *One Land—Many Cultures: Archaeological Studies in Honour of Stanislao Loffreda OFM*, edited by Giovanni Claudio Bottini, L. Di Segni, and Leslaw Daniel Chrupcala, 245-57. Jerusalem: Franciscan Printing Press, 2003.

Martyr, Justin. "Dialogue of Justin with Trypho, a Jew." In *The Apostolic Fathers with Justin Martyr and Irenaeus,* edited by Alexander Roberts, James Donaldson, and A. Cleveland Coxe. Vol. 1. The Ante-Nicene Fathers, 194-270. Buffalo, NY: The Christian Literature Company, 1885.

Mazar, Eilat. *The Palace of King David: Excavations at the Summit of the City of David: Preliminary Report of the Seasons 2005-2007.* Jerusalem: Shoham Academic Research and Publication, 2009.

Mazar, Eilat. *Discovering the Solomonic Wall in Jerusalem: A Remarkable Archaeological Adventure.* Jerusalem: Shoham Academic Research and Publication, 2011.

Mazar, Eilat, Yiftah Shalev, Irit Yezerski, and Reut Livyatan Ben-Arie. *The Summit of the City of David, Excavations 2005-2008: Final Reports Volume I.* Jerusalem: Shoham Academic Research and Publication, 2015.

Nuseibeh, Saïd and Oleg Grabar. *The Dome of the Rock.* London: Thames and Hudson, 1996.

Origen. "Origen against Celsus." In *Fathers of the Third Century: Tertullian, Part Fourth; Minucius Felix; Commodian; Origen, Parts First and Second,* edited by Alexander Roberts, James Donaldson, and A. Cleveland Coxe, translated by Frederick Crombie, Vol. 4, The Ante-Nicene Fathers, 395-669. Buffalo, New York: The Christian Literature Publishing Company, 1885.

Peters, F. E. *Jerusalem: The Holy City in the Eyes of Chroniclers, Visitors, Pilgrims, and Prophets from the Days of Abraham to the Beginnings of Modern Times.* Princeton, NJ: Princeton University Press, 1985.

Pfeiffer, Charles F. *Wycliffe Dictionary of Biblical Archaeology.* Peabody, MA: Hendrickson Publishers, 2000.

Pixner, Bargil. "Church of the Apostles Found on Mount Zion." *Biblical Archaeology Review* XVI, no. 3, May/June (1990): 16-35, 60.

Rainey, Anson F. and R. Steven Notley. *The Sacred Bridge: Carta's Atlas of the Biblical World.* Jerusalem: Carta, 2006.

Saller, Sylvester. "Iron Age Remains from the Site of a New School at Bethlehem." *Liber Annus* 18 (1968): 153-80.

Shanks, Hershel. "The Tombs of Silwan." *Biblical Archaeology Review* 20, no. 3, May/June (1994): 39-51.

Tacitus. *Annals of Tacitus.* Translated by A. J. Church and W. J. Brodribb. London: Macmillan and Co., 1876.

Taylor, Joan E. *Christians and the Holy Places: The Myth of Jewish-Christian Origins.* Oxford: Clarendon Press, 1993.

The Talmud: A Selection. Edited and translated by Norman Solomon. London: Penguin, 2009.

Vincent, Hugues and F. M. Abel. *Bethléem, Le Sanctuaire De La Nativité.* Edited by J. Gabalda. Paris: Librairie Victor Lecoffre, 1914.

Vincent, L. H. "L'église De L'éléona." *Revue Biblique (1892-1940)* 7, no. 4 (1910): 573-74.

Vincent, L. H., E. J. H. Mackay, and F. M. Abel. *Hébron: Le Haram El-Khalîl: Sépulture Des Patriarches*. Paris: Ernest Leroux, 1923.

Weill, Raymond and L. H. Vincent. *The City of David: Revisiting Early Excavations; English Translations of Reports by Raymond Weill and L. H. Vincent*. Edited by Hershel Shanks. Washington, D.C.: Biblical Archaeology Society, 2004.

Wilkenson, John. "Constantinian Churches in Palestine." In *Ancient Churches Revealed*, edited by Yoram Tsafrir, 23-27. Jerusalem: Israel Exploration Society, 1993.

TOPIC INDEX

ABOUT JOEL KRAMER

Having pursued many interests in the course of his life, Joel has compiled a varied resumé: expeditioner, photo journalist, pastor, film producer, and archaeologist.

While living in Jerusalem for almost ten years, Joel earned an M.A. in archaeology from the University of the Holy Land. He was fortunate to be able to study under world-renowned archaeologist Dr. Shimon Gibson. Participating in numerous digs, Joel gained valuable field experience working on excavations in Jerusalem, Bethlehem, and Ai.

Currently, Joel lives with his wife, Cathy, and their three children in Amman, Jordan. He continues to write, research and pursue archaeological interests, particularly as an in-the-field adjunct professor for Shepherds Theological Seminary in Cary, NC.

A former pastor as well as a seasoned archaeologist, Joel takes his readers into the world of the Bible—its people, places, and events—and uses archaeology to demonstrate the historicity of those people, places, and events. Beyond validating the biblical record, however, Joel aims to bring clarity to the reality that together, scripture and archaeology highlight mankind's need of redemption and God's presence and work through the course of human history.

Joel's passion for the Bible comes through in his teaching, but his style is not to simply "tell you what to think." Instead, he lays out context and provides primary sources and equips his readers/listeners to think for themselves. Those who experience Joel's writing, speaking, and teaching find themselves stirred by the Bible's profound truth and equipped to explain why they trust it.

For more information about joining a Bible study tour or to contact Joel:

www.ExpeditionBible.com